Ff

Sharon Sadako Takeda and Kaye Durland Spilker

PREFACE BY
John Galliano

ESSAY BY
Kimberly Chrisman-Campbell

AND CONTRIBUTIONS BY
Kimberly Chrisman-Campbell
Clarissa M. Esguerra
Nicole LaBouff

FASHIONING *fashion*

EUROPEAN DRESS IN DETAIL 1700–1915

LOS ANGELES COUNTY MUSEUM OF ART

DELMONICO BOOKS · PRESTEL

MUNICH BERLIN LONDON NEW YORK

THIS PUBLICATION IS DEDICATED TO THE GENEROUS DONORS LISTED BELOW, WHOSE MUNIFICENT CONTRIBUTIONS MADE THE MUSEUM'S RECENT ACQUISITION OF A MAJOR EUROPEAN COSTUME COLLECTION POSSIBLE. ALL ILLUSTRATED DRESS AND ACCESSORIES PRESENTED IN THIS VOLUME, EXCEPT WHERE OTHERWISE NOTED, ARE PART OF THIS MAGNANIMOUS GIFT.

Suzanne A. Saperstein

Michael and Ellen Michelson

WITH ADDITIONAL FUNDING FROM
Costume Council, LACMA
Edgerton Foundation
Gail and Gerald Oppenheimer
Maureen H. Shapiro
Grace Tsao
Lenore and Richard Wayne

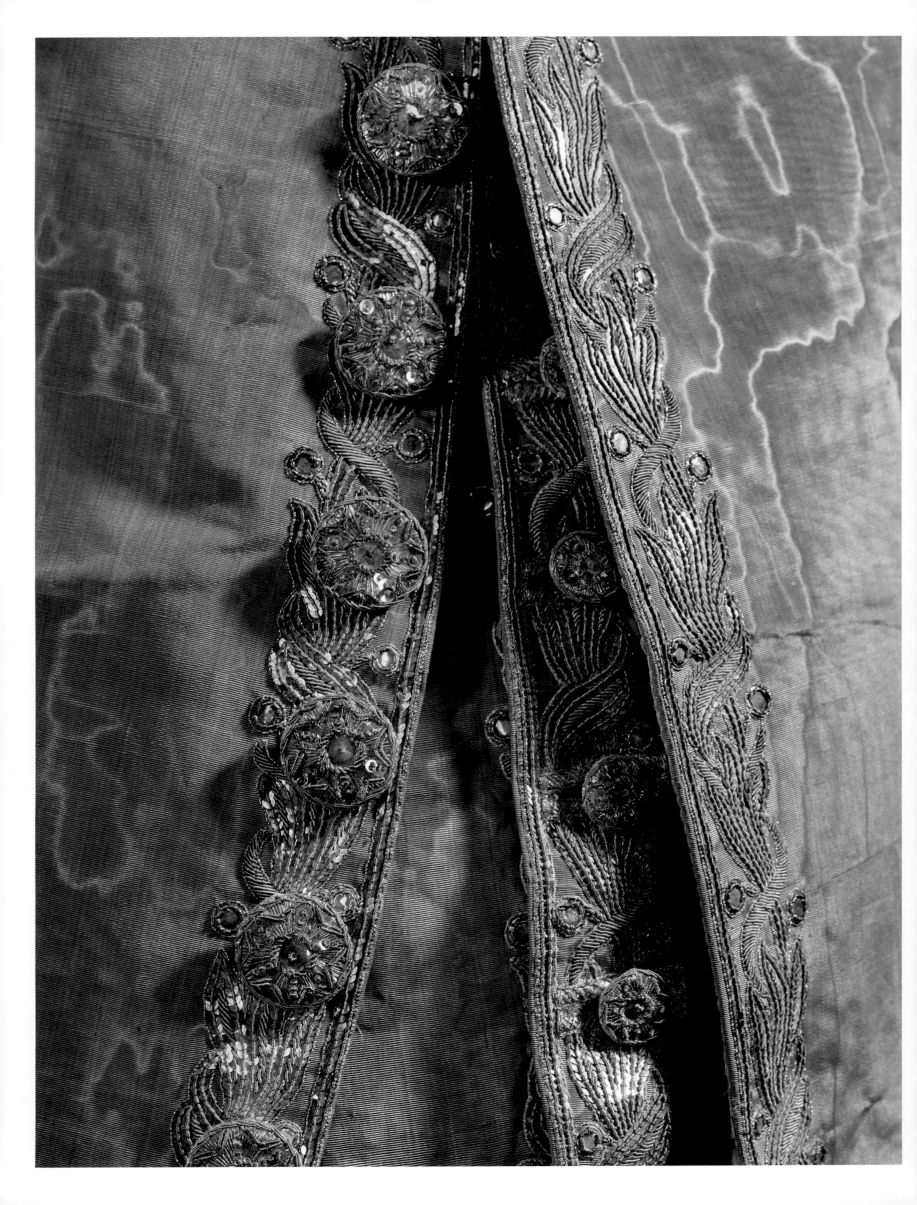

DIRECTOR'S FOREWORD

Fashioning Fashion: European Dress in Detail, 1700–1915 is the first project to highlight a major collection of European men's, women's, and children's dress and accessories acquired by the Los Angeles County Museum of Art in 2007. Selections from this important recent acquisition have been skillfully integrated with objects from the holdings of LACMA's internationally respected Costume and Textiles Department to produce Fashioning Fashion. The exhibition, and this accompanying book, concentrates on the details of creating fashionable dress from the Age of Enlightenment to World War I.

Organized by senior curator and department head Sharon Sadako Takeda and curator Kaye Durland Spilker, with the collaboration of research scholar Kimberly Chrisman-Campbell, curatorial assistant Clarissa Esguerra, and Wallis Annenberg curatorial fellow Nicole LaBouff, Fashioning Fashion is arranged in four thematic sections: Timeline, Textiles, Tailoring, and Trim. Addressing the fundamentals of making fashion, the sections include objects that illustrate the ever-changing stylish silhouette: a rich assortment of textiles, expert tailoring techniques, and decorative trimmings utilized in European dress from 1700 to 1915. These same elements continue to motivate contemporary haute couture designers, including John Galliano, who in the preface of this publication eloquently writes about the process of creating fashion.

In today's world, where the lines between paintings, sculpture, media, and design are blurring, it is a great moment to be considering the enormous importance of dress, especially within the context of an encyclopedic art museum. This is why there was no hesitation in making the new European costume collection—expertly assembled over fifty years collectively by Martin Kamer and Wolfgang Ruf—one of my first major art initiatives after arriving at LACMA in April 2006.

This landmark acquisition catapults LACMA's holdings of European costume to the highest category of quality. I am proud of this decision and privileged that Suzanne A. Saperstein and Michael and Ellen Michelson had the conviction and passion to make possible the most ambitious initiative for the Costume and Textiles Department in LACMA's history. We are extremely indebted to them and grateful for the additional support from the Costume Council, the Edgerton Foundation, Gail and Gerald Oppenheimer, Maureen H. Shapiro, Grace Tsao, and Lenore and Richard Wayne.

Finally reaching a level of maturity worthy of a major art museum after decades of steadfast support from the museum's Costume Council and numerous individual donors, LACMA now becomes an important destination for European costume studies. We are indebted to all of our benefactors for ensuring that intellectually stimulating projects such as Fashioning Fashion can draw from a world-class permanent collection and inspire future generations.

Michael Govan
CEO AND WALLIS ANNENBERG DIRECTOR
LOS ANGELES COUNTY MUSEUM OF ART

PREFACE

I was very excited when I visited the Los Angeles County Museum of Art in April 2009 for a sneak preview of its upcoming exhibition *Fashioning Fashion: European Dress in Detail, 1700–1915*, and I am honored to write this preface. When researching or creating a collection, it is the details, the stories, and the history behind the work that never cease to inspire me. In the process of design, it is that tiny nip, or tuck, or invisible hook and eye that can magically transform an entire silhouette. Those are the ingredients I care about. You see, I always want to know every single detail and idea, right down to the very last stitch. Every detail matters, whether you are telling a story or creating a collection or starting a revolution. This exhibition will take you through fashion and time with the sumptuous variety of an extraordinary collection. I promise, it cannot fail to inspire you.

I was particularly taken with a gentleman's vest (left and p. 154–155); it is simply *charmant* (charming), to quote the coquettish collar. The piece dates back to the eighteenth century and the time of the French Revolution, an era I have always found to be a rich source of inspiration. You can spend hours studying this vest. It gives many clues about the turbulent time, weaving style with politics, rebellion, and the *tricolore*. Here fashion speaks its owner's mind through intricate needlework and beauty rather than through the violence of the day. As well as the collar, other clues can be found on the pockets. One is the phrase, "L'HABIT NE FAIT PAS LE MOINE" ("The habit does not make the monk"), a caution to never judge a book by its cover or, indeed, take things, such as fashion, and its wearer, on face value alone. The other pocket reads, "HONI SOIT QUI MAL Y PENSE," a motto I recognized from the English Order of the Garter, which originally comes from the Old French saying, "Shame upon him who thinks evil of it." Powerful messages to carry on your person! It is genius. I love the hidden messages and use of heroic symbolism and dandy analogy to, quite literally, wear your loyalties on your chest. For me fashion is there to empower, but you can also play with it, and use it to disguise and conceal. This vest is a brilliant example of all this. It also serves as a strong visual reminder to always look past the frosting and seek the person within.

So, why don't you look even closer at that vest? There are still many clues to unravel. Through its design and embroidery it tells how the wealthy once dressed like caterpillars by day, ostentatious butterflies by night, but then had to remember their loyalty to the state, to the blue, white, and red. This wearer is, as the collar hints, a bit of a charmer and seems to play it safe and profess both loyalties. Take the tiny lapels: they are embroidered, one with a shorn caterpillar, the other with a butterfly with its wings cut. Does this mean the wearer's wings have been cut? Or is he glad that the rich, with their decadent ways, have been stopped? Well, this he can debate whichever way the company prefers....

I wish I had been commissioned to design this vest; it is a masterpiece of fashion and function as well as showing sadness, sympathy, beauty, and wit. The vest is both a political and a fashion statement that captures the mood at the beginning of a new era. It also shows how style reacted, like a fickle mirror, and instantly rejected the gaudy finery so beloved before. This vest says so much more than a first glance can glean, and it is just one example of what you will find in this exhibition. It is objects like this that make my job so exciting.

Fashion's spirit is ever changing and ever challenging you to keep up. The constant shift is what fascinates and inspires me, and adds color and character to the narrative of the pieces. Fashion exists to capture a moment, to transcend language, culture, class, and time. But fashion must also guard secrets: of the figure, of hopes and dreams. It is the ultimate barometer of the then and the now. Eras can be defined by what we wore as much as by who we were, so we must design pieces as inventive as this vest to capture every chameleon and butterfly.

I want to inspire and push fashion forward, to celebrate the beauty of the past as much as the beauty of today. I hope that you enjoy this exhibition as much as I have.

John Galliano

INTRODUCTION

Sharon Sadako Takeda

Fashioning a collection of European dress and accessories began in 1915 at the Los Angeles County Museum of History, Science, and Art, a year before the fledgling institution acquired its first painting and a half-century before the art division splintered off to create the Los Angeles County Museum of Art (LACMA). Since the formation of the Costume and Textiles Department in 1953, several generations of curators have strategically expanded and exhibited its permanent collection, which now represents more than one hundred cultures and two thousand years of human creativity in the textile and fashion arts.

At the end of 2005, LACMA received documentation on a major European fashion collection assembled by two of the foremost dealers in the field: Martin Kamer of London, England, and Wolfgang Ruf of Beckenried, Switzerland. Both have dealt in historic textiles and dress for more than twenty-five years, each building an impressive international client list of museums, including LACMA, while often reserving select pieces for their own private collections. Competitors for many years, Kamer and Ruf in the twilight of their careers found it more and more challenging to locate high-quality historic fashionable dress. The two decided to merge their respective costume collections and offer it as one to select international museums. Representing a total of fifty years of acquisitions through active bidding at auctions and estate sales as well as through purchases and trades with other dealers, their collaboration resulted in a stellar collection of fashion and accessories for men, women, and children that would be difficult, if not impossible, to replicate today.

The addition of the Kamer-Ruf Collection to any museum would be a coup simply for its breadth and depth, but even more significantly for its overall quality and number of extremely rare pieces, including a man's vest intricately embroidered with powerful messages relevant to the French Revolution (pp. 8, 154–155) and a feathered, bejeweled turban by the famed French fashion designer Paul Poiret worn by his wife and muse, Denise, at his legendary "Thousand and Second Night" party in June 1911 (p. 176). For LACMA the acquisition of this extraordinary collection—with strong examples of fashion from France, England, the Netherlands, and the Iberian Peninsula, as well as Asian

exports for the Western market—instantly strengthened the museum's already respectable European dress collection, which had been built, almost piece by piece, by the generosity of the museum's Costume Council and individual donors.

Soon after his arrival at LACMA in April 2006, CEO and Wallis Annenberg Director Michael Govan challenged curators from every department to be fearless in their pursuit of possible art acquisitions and to find objects or collections that would greatly alter the museum's permanent collection and art-world profile. The Costume and Textiles Department presented the Kamer-Ruf Collection for the Director's consideration. Govan understood the importance of costume for an encyclopedic art museum such as LACMA: not only did it enliven and add dimension to paintings and sculpture, but the relatively recent elevation of the role of fashion among art historians and contemporary art curators also made its place in the museum essential. After examining the collection in Basel, Switzerland, he made the Kamer-Ruf Collection one of his first major art-acquisition initiatives.

This impressive agenda was bolstered by a munificent gift from Michael and Ellen Michelson immediately after Ellen's viewing of the collection in Basel with Govan. Additional generous contributions followed from the museum's Costume Council, the Edgerton Foundation, Gail and Gerald Oppenheimer, Maureen H. Shapiro, Grace Tsao, and Lenore and Richard Wayne. A final grand contribution from Suzanne A. Saperstein secured the collection for LACMA, instantly raising the museum's European fashion collection to a significantly higher level.

Fashioning Fashion: European Dress in Detail, 1700–1915 is the inaugural presentation of this newly acquired gift. The exhibition and this publication celebrate the acquisition milestone and, by integrating key examples collected over the life span of the museum, also acknowledge the enduring legacy of generous donors who have actively participated in fashioning a world-class collection for LACMA.

In deciding which objects to exhibit, pieces were thoughtfully chosen for their respective roles in the story of fashion's aesthetic and technical development from the Age of Enlightenment to World War I. Organized in four thematic sections—Timeline,

Textiles, Tailoring, and Trim—the exhibition examines the sweeping changes that occurred in fashionable dress from 1700 to 1915 (the period of time represented by the art objects in the new acquisition), providing an in-depth look at the details of luxurious textiles, exacting tailoring techniques, and lush trimmings.

The Timeline section offers a chronological panorama of female and male fashions. The women's visual timeline is illustrated with dresses in various shades of white in order to focus attention on the evolving fashionable silhouette—how each successive era emphasized a different part of the human anatomy and changed the position of waistlines and hemlines. By contrast, the men's timeline begins with colorful examples that showcase how eighteenth-century aristocratic men rivaled their female counterparts in the desire to impress with dress, and concludes with a subdued 1911 pinstripe suit, a harbinger of the business suit that has remained relatively unchanged for a century.

The fashioning of fashion begins with the choice of fabric by medium, weight, color, and occasionally pattern. An assortment of textiles—from silk to cotton, gauze to velvet, plain to printed—is highlighted in the Textiles section. The simple interlacing of a vertical warp in one color and a horizontal weft in another color creates an iridescent plain-weave fabric that, when made into a garment, appears to change color as the wearer moves. Eighteenth-century aristocratic garments made from such "changeable" or "shot" silks (pp. 48–49, 74–75) were particularly striking as courtiers maneuvered around candlelit rooms. After the French Revolution, the craze for fashions that mimicked the flowing and revealing drapery characteristic of ancient Greek and Roman statues resulted in a huge demand for gossamer cotton muslin. Raw cotton from various European colonies that had become widely available in the second half of the eighteenth century helped meet the growing demand for cotton yardage. Similar in transparency yet more complicated and time-consuming to produce, cotton gauze (pp. 52–53) was an understated lavish expenditure for the most discerning fashion-conscious consumer. Equally thin and lightweight, exotic cashmere shawls woven of the finest goat-fleece underdown (pp. 37 left, 53) provided both warmth and luxury to diaphanous neoclassical dresses. Imported woven silks from China (p. 58) and printed, resist-dyed, and mordant-painted cottons from India constructed into stylish European creations demonstrated exotic subdued elegance appreciated by the cognoscenti. Exoticism in the form of the imagined Far East is seen in "bizarre" (p. 54), chinoiserie (pp. 57–58), and Japanese-inspired (pp. 46, 51) patterned silks produced in Europe. Sumptuous silk velvets were perennial fashion favorites for both men and women. Some well-dressed nineteenth-century men owned hundreds of richly patterned silk and silk-velvet vests that added colorful expression to their somber suits (pp. 60–61).

Throughout the eighteenth century, new designs for dress fabrics emerged with each change of season. The fabrication of lavish textiles by hand on drawlooms was labor intensive and therefore expensive. Even with technical innovations, such as the perfection of the Jacquard loom attachment in 1801 (which allowed for increasingly complex patterns to be woven semi-mechanically), fabric often remained the costliest feature of high fashion. Textiles were treasured—and made into stylish clothing that was passed down to loved ones and often refashioned into more updated styles.

The manipulation of textiles through cutting, stitching, and padding in order to sculpt three-dimensional garments that conformed to the idealized shape or fashionable silhouette of each era is explored in the Tailoring section. In the eighteenth century, lengths of expensive fabric were used efficiently with little waste. Cut into few pattern pieces, garments were hand-stitched. Suit jackets for men were unpadded, while dresses were given volume with the aid of wide hoop petticoats known as *paniers* (p. 77). During the nineteenth century, with the advancement of tailoring tools and techniques, styles changed in dramatic ways, accentuating or minimizing different body parts—shoulders, breasts, waist, hips, derriere—in ongoing attempts to keep up with fashion.

By the mid-nineteenth century, the invention and widespread use of the sewing machine permitted a faster method of assembling the growing number of multiple pieces of fabric, and spawned the creation of more complicated three-dimensional forms. Men's suit jackets were cut short in front but gave way to long tails; lapels were strategically cut and stitched to ensure a smooth transition from the collar; and the body of the jacket was padded in various key locations—shoulder, underarm, and chest. Female garments composed from myriad shaped fabric pieces fit over a variety of understructures from corsets to cage crinolines and bustles that gave rise to correspondingly exaggerated fashionable silhouettes.

The decoration of a garment enhanced the beauty and appreciation of fashion. The combination of rich materials and time-consuming hand techniques often contributed to making the cost of trimmings higher than the price of the garment's textile or tailoring. And, like expensive jewelry, elaborate trimmings indicated wealth and social position.

The artistry of embroiderers, quilters, and lace makers is undeniable when examining the details of the elegantly embellished garments in the Trim section. Eighteenth-century examples, such as the realistic depiction of flowering plants embroidered on a man's velvet suit (p. 128), the subtle texture of white-on-white corded quilting punctuated with embroidered knots on a woman's stomacher (p. 139), and the delicate handmade linen lace accessories (pp. 156–157), surely delighted the wearers while enticing members of their aristocratic circles to draw near for a closer look. In the nineteenth century, as inventive manufacturing techniques successfully imitated hand techniques, trimmings as well as fashionable dress became more affordable to the growing European middle class.

Fashioning Fashion offers a wonderful opportunity to examine the transformation of fashion over a span of more than two centuries, as well as providing historical context to show how political events, technical innovations, and global trade often profoundly affected style. Because eighteenth- and nineteenth-century fashion moved more slowly than the lightning-speed pace of contemporary fashion, great attention could be paid to the smallest of details. It is little wonder that many of today's top haute couture designers often look to the past in order to find meaning in the present. The intriguing and inspiring examples of historic dress found in *Fashioning Fashion* are as captivating today as they were centuries ago.

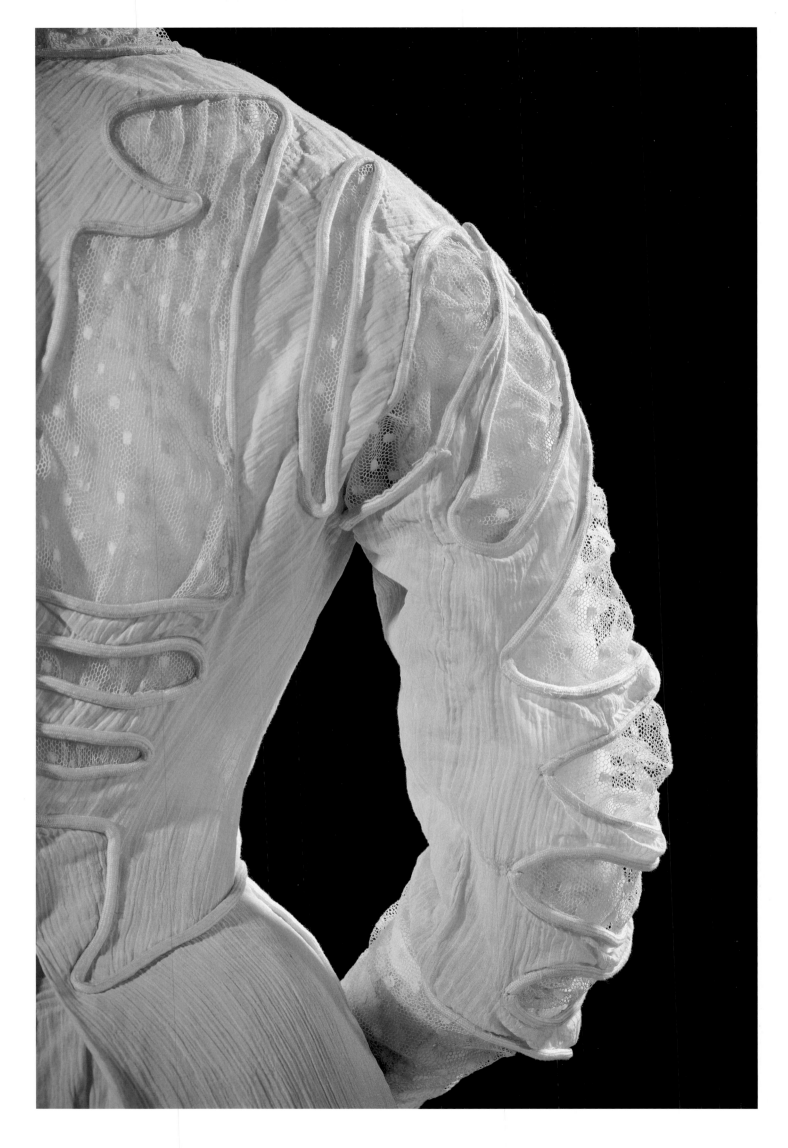

Fashioning (and Refashioning) European Fashion

Kimberly Chrisman-Campbell

THE PERIOD 1700 TO 1915 WAS AN ERA OF TREMENDOUS CHANGE and heterogeneity in Europe. The fashions of the times record the social history of a world transformed by revolution and industrialization, a world clinging to an idealized past even as it embraced modern technology. European society was dominated by the court and the aristocracy, though a swiftly growing middle class increasingly challenged these traditional arbiters of taste and fashion. After a period of relative stability, a succession of wars and revolutions in the nineteenth century shifted borders and allegiances, culminating in World War I. Exploration and trade led to greater contact between Europe and Asia and the Middle East. Industrialization transformed the way goods were made, marketed, and purchased. Manufacturing replaced agriculture as Europe's economic stronghold. And women took small, steady steps toward liberation; however, it was only during World War I that they entered the workforce in significant numbers and won the right to vote. These history lessons can be read in the smallest details of fashion.

Between the eighteenth and twentieth centuries, the world began to feel much smaller. Throughout Europe, trade expansion and an explosion in publishing eroded regional distinctions, including distinctions in dress. Advances in transportation and communication arrived in particularly rapid succession toward the end of the nineteenth century: bicycles, cars, and airplanes compressed distances, while telephones and radios eliminated them altogether. International trade expositions and world's fairs introduced Europeans to new cultures and peoples, as well as to new inventions and technologies. The cultural, geographic, and sartorial gaps between East and West no longer seemed insurmountable.

Indeed, the more we delve into the history of fashion in the eighteenth and nineteenth centuries, the more familiar it looks. This period witnessed the birth of the fashion industry as we know it today—that is, seasonal, international, and corporate. Then as now, fashion was a major domestic and export business in Europe, centered in Paris but drawing clients, craftsmen, and materials from around the world. Mass production and ready-to-wear clothing were being pioneered on a small scale, though the technologies necessary to realize their full potential were still evolving. The first modern department stores opened in the 1830s, selling a wide variety of goods under one roof, at fixed prices. Concepts like fashion revivals, globalization, and "green" fashion are not new; they are part of a continuous cycle of fashioning and refashioning that dates back to the beginning of the eighteenth century, when traditional barriers to fashionability—geographic, socioeconomic, and technological—began to unravel, and fashion was transformed from an aristocratic social duty to a pop-culture phenomenon.

FROM THE SEVENTEENTH CENTURY ON, France was the epicenter of the fashion world. The formidable combination of Paris fashions and Lyon silks—plus a host of subsidiary manufacturers, organized into a highly efficient, government-regulated guild system—set the course of European fashion. As Jean-Baptiste Colbert (1619–1683), finance minister to Louis XIV (1638–1715), put it: "Fashions were to France what the mines of Peru were to Spain"—that is, an extremely lucrative domestic and export commodity.[1]

Historically, fashion has been a major economic force in France, but it was only in the eighteenth century that it began to be regarded as something more than a mere trade. "The work of fashion is an art," wrote journalist Louis-Sébastien Mercier (1740–1814). "Darling, triumphant art, which, in this century, has received honors and distinctions. This art enters into the palace of kings, where it receives a flattering welcome."[2]

The death of Louis XIV in 1715 prompted a revolution in taste. The grand, formal portraits and ponderous allegorical works of art that had celebrated the reign of the Sun King fell out of fashion in favor of intimate, lighthearted paintings in delicate pastel colors. Rococo art, as it would become known, was criticized as being unnatural, frivolous, and morally corrupting. But its admirers were attracted to its escapist sentimentality, its theatricality, and its emphasis on ornament, all of which translated easily into fashion. The art of tailoring (loosely defined as cutting and sewing) lost prestige as fashion's focus shifted from the structure of dress to its surface.

fig. 2
Suit (detail)
France, 1780–85
Page 197

Because the fundamental outer garments—the three-piece suit for men and the three-piece ensemble of dress, petticoat, and stomacher for women—remained the same from the early to late eighteenth century, with only minor and gradual changes in cut and construction, the most conspicuous developments in fashion for that period were superficial. Getting dressed required many separate garments, accessories, and ornaments that could be taken apart and rearranged, mixed and matched according to the wearer's taste (fig. 1). Trimmings and accessories were pinned, tied, or basted onto a basic garment, which was made of high-quality fabric but did not necessarily entail complex cutting or sewing techniques.

It was these trimmings and accessories that determined whether or not a person was in style, and often were even more costly than the textiles they adorned. Such trimmings and accessories were designed to be recycled for maximum value and visual impact. Lace (worn by men as well as women) was handmade and could cost as much as jewels; and like jewels, lace was passed down from generation to generation. Instead of being permanently attached to garments, lace could be removed, rearranged, and reused. Metallic trimmings, such as gold braid or lace, contained real gold and were sold by weight rather than length. Court dresses and suits were heavily embroidered with real gold and silver thread. Many such examples from the eighteenth century did not survive, as they were burned to salvage the precious metals. Other suits that appeared to be embroidered were simply appliquéd with embroidered strips of fabric (fig. 2 and pp. 192–195, 197) that could be removed and reapplied to other garments. Detachable buttons and buckles decorated coats, waistcoats, breeches, and shoes (pp. 181–183). Interchangeable accessories, like stomachers and cuffs, could thus serve several different garments. Even women's pockets were detachable, worn on a ribbon under the petticoat and accessed through slits in the dress seams.

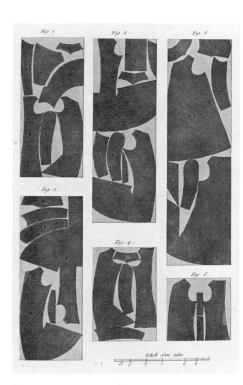

fig. 3
Denis Diderot
Tailleur d'Habits et Tailleur de Corps,
pl. XII (detail), 1776
Etching on paper
Doris Stein Research Center, LACMA

fig. 4
François Boucher
Madame de Pompadour, 1759
Oil on canvas
By kind permission of the Trustees of the
Wallace Collection, London

fig. 5 (opposite)
Vivienne Westwood
*Prêt-à-porter collection for autumn/winter 1995–96,
Paris, France*

In the eighteenth century, clothing was a major financial investment. Not only were trimmings costly, but textiles were woven on man-powered looms, and all sewing was done by hand. There were few ready-to-wear garments, no designer knockoffs, no inexpensive man-made substitutes for silk and wool, the principal fibers used in outerwear. Everyone wore the real thing, whether it was new or heavily used. Cotton became widely available in Europe in the second half of the eighteenth century, but because it was a novelty, and one that had to be imported from far-flung colonies, it was still fairly expensive. So while labor was plentiful and inexpensive, textiles were not. Carefully illustrated trade manuals showed tailors and dressmakers how to cut pattern pieces so as not to waste a single scrap of fabric (fig. 3). Thus, the cost of a garment was determined by the quality of its textiles more than by the skill (or fame) of its maker.

All clothing was expensive, but fashionable clothing was an extraordinary luxury. In the eighteenth century, fashionable clothing had a fixed and finite life span. After a piece went out of fashion, it was given to a servant or sold to a secondhand-clothes dealer who might clean, alter, or update the garment before reselling it. This cycle of redistribution continued until the garment was not just hopelessly outdated but threadbare as well.

In light of this routine recycling of eighteenth-century garments, it is extraordinary that any survived intact. The fact that many examples are still with us in the twenty-first century is a powerful testament to their astounding beauty. The elegance and excess of the eighteenth century—personified by such stylish heroines as Madame de Pompadour (1721–1764) (fig. 4) and Marie Antoinette (1755–1793)—continue to inspire fashion designers today (fig. 5).

THOUGH ALL OF EUROPE LOOKED TO FRANCE FOR FASHION in the eighteenth century, other countries—near and far—impacted European fashion to an extent that may seem surprising today, considering the relatively limited transportation and communication methods of the era. The restrained, sober sophistication of English sportswear provided a perfect counterbalance to French formality and love of ornament. The English defined the natural shape of the body rather than distorting it, and popularized practical, comfortable garments designed for country living and physical activity. For men, these included the frock coat and riding boots. Women adopted the fitted *robe à l'anglaise* (pp. 36 right, 78) and the riding habit, fashions ideally worn with unpowdered hair and a natural complexion, in the English style. By 1786 *The Fashionable Magazine* could boast, "London now, generally speaking, gives Fashions to Paris and, of course, to all Europe, not Paris to London."[3]

China has been trading with the West since the time of the Roman Empire, and luxurious textiles formed an important part of this commerce. In fact, by the late nineteenth century, the network of overland trade routes was dubbed the Silk Road. Even after Europeans penetrated the secrets of sericulture and began to develop their own silk industry in the twelfth century, imported Chinese textiles—whether woven (p. 58), embroidered (p. 141), or painted—remained perennially fashionable and prestigious. Similarly, under the general label "chinoiserie," Chinese porcelain, lacquer, architecture, and interior design captivated Europe.

India was another rich source of imports and inspiration. The Dutch and British East India Companies started trading Indian textiles in the early seventeenth century. In the late 1790s, soldiers in the service of Emperor Napoléon Bonaparte (1769–1821) brought cashmere shawls home from their campaigns in Egypt, where they had encountered Indian traders.

Other commercial and colonial connections also played significant roles in shaping European dress: the American colonies provided cotton for Britain, and the French imported it from their colonies in the West Indies. Through these mercantile and diplomatic channels, Europeans absorbed foreign textile techniques and motifs in addition to the textiles themselves.

fig. 6
Robert-Jacques Lefèvre
*Portrait of a Woman Holding a Pencil and a
Drawing Book*, c. 1808
Oil on canvas
Gift of Joan Palevsky, LACMA

fig. 7
Jean-Auguste-Dominique Ingres
Portrait of Mme. de Senonnes, 1814
Oil on canvas
Musée des Beaux-Arts de Nantes, France

However, these foreign goods usually were made for export, and their exoticism was translated into a safe, recognizably European context. Embroidered Chinese textiles, American muslins, and Indian chintzes were fashioned into Western-style dresses, petticoats, and waistcoats. With a few notable exceptions, like the banyan—a voluminous robe with a front opening, adopted as a man's dressing gown in Europe (pp. 58, 65)—it was Asian textiles, not Asian garments, that appealed to European consumers. Few could tell the difference between a Chinese garment and an Indian or Turkish one; all were labeled "Oriental" or "Asiatic." These exotic styles were worn together—regardless of geographic origin—by European men and women hoping to appear progressive and picturesque.

EYEWITNESSES COMPARED THE FRENCH REVOLUTION OF 1789 to an earthquake or a hurricane, and its rupture certainly was of such magnitude and violence that its repercussions were felt around the world, and for decades afterward. The Revolution threw France's government, economy, and social structure into chaos, and permanently altered not only fashion production but the meaning of fashion itself.

In those violent and uncertain times, fashion began to look backward to an idealized past. While fashion revivals had existed earlier in the eighteenth century, they became more frequent and vigorous in the wake of the Revolution. Neoclassicism—the revival of ancient Greek and Roman art forms and aesthetics that had begun in the mid-eighteenth century with the excavations of the ruins of Pompeii and Herculaneum—became more refined and historically accurate as France embraced the democratic politics and philosophies of those lost civilizations. High waistlines, body-conscious silhouettes, and flowing diaphanous fabrics imitated the clinging drapery of classical statuary (fig. 6 and pp. 37 left, 53). Women collected cashmere shawls not because they came from India but because they looked Grecian. The visual and material excesses characteristic of eighteenth-century fashion were deemed politically incorrect, relics of feudalism and despotism.

Although France spent the next decade at war with its European neighbors—hereditary monarchies that could not sit idly by while the French overthrew and, ultimately, killed their own king—Paris continued to dictate fashion throughout the Western world. Styles that had originated as political statements became appreciated for their own merits, removed from their French roots.

Historical references and revivals, such as neoclassicism, became hallmarks of fashion in the nineteenth century. As ongoing warfare and the technologies born of the Industrial Revolution transformed the natural and sociopolitical landscape of Europe, people sought comfort and continuity in the familiar yet otherworldly fashions of bygone days. Again and again, fashion revisited the past, reinterpreting its glories and beauties for contemporary tastes. Along with fashion revivals, elaborate masquerade balls and meticulously researched productions of historical plays and operas offered psychological escape from the evils of the modern world.

Fashion revivals offered something for everyone, regardless of their political persuasion. Napoléon borrowed elements of his imperial costume and regalia from historical sources as diverse as ancient Rome, the fifth-century King Childeric (circa 440–481), and Charlemagne (742–814), blending classical and French history to present an entirely fictional yet thoroughly convincing display of power. His wife, Josephine (1763–1814), wore neoclassical white dresses with high waistlines, a silhouette still known as the "Empire line." With the fall of Napoléon and the restoration of the French monarchy in 1814, fashion looked back to the days of King Henri IV (1553–1610), a golden age in French history, and one that King Louis XVIII (1755–1824), newly returned from exile, was eager to re-create. Elements of medieval and Renaissance dress, including paned and puffed sleeves, long veils, plumed hats, and rufflike collars (figs. 7, 8), entered the fashionable female's wardrobe. Luxurious trimmings and accessories like embroidery, fur, jewels, and lace returned to favor. These new historical references joined and eventually eclipsed the ancient Greek and Roman influences typical of the Revolutionary period.

fig. 8
Jacket (Spencer) (detail)
France, c. 1815
Page 84

IRONICALLY, CONSCIOUS EFFORTS TO HISTORICIZE FASHION led to several innovations in clothing and textile production. As Europe's agricultural economy gave way to an industrial one, technology transformed the manufacturing and marketing of clothing and textiles. The first attempts at mechanizing textile and clothing production were made in the eighteenth century, but their impact was not widely felt until the nineteenth century. The Jacquard loom attachment, perfected in 1801, made it possible to create intricately patterned textiles cheaply, regardless of the skill of the weaver, using a punch card system (widely recognized today as the precursor of the computer). Soon, not just weaving but also spinning, printing, embroidery, and sewing could be done quickly and inexpensively by machine, which greatly reduced the cost of clothing and textiles.

New, patented products made with modern materials permitted ever-greater distortions of the female body. Metal eyelets were invented in 1828, making it possible to lace corsets very tightly without the risk of ripping the fabric; the artificially slender waist became one of the most distinctive and enduring features of nineteenth-century womenswear. In 1848 the slot-and-stud corset fastening was patented (p. 114). Using this quick-opening corset, a woman could undress herself without the help of a servant; adjustable laces in back controlled the shape and size of the torso. The sewing machine, which was patented in 1846, allowed for more pieces of fabric and thus a more accurate, contoured fit. Steam-molding on metal or ceramic forms produced a tight-fitting hourglass shape without the need for precise measurements. The sewing machine also could handle leather and other durable fabrics needed for tight lacing.

fig. 9
Pretty Catch, January 1, 1860
Hulton Archive, London Stereoscopic Company
Comic Series—504

fig. 10
Arkadius, *London Fashion Week, Autumn/Winter 2004–2005 at the BFC Tent on 16 February 2004—Day 3*

Crinolines (and, later, bustles) took advantage of the same new technologies as corsets. The word *crinoline* originally meant horsehair (*crin* in French) woven with linen (*lin*). It was applied to the rigid petticoats adopted in the early 1850s to support the voluminous skirts then in fashion. Subsequent experiments with cane and inflatable tubes (fig. 9) were quickly abandoned in favor of skeletal hoops made of flexible steel springs, patented in 1856. These so-called cage crinolines were lightweight and easy to maneuver, and provided a comfortable and hygienic alternative to layers of thick petticoats. They were so popular that by 1866 it was estimated that England's steelmaking capital, Sheffield, was producing one hundred tons of crinoline steel per week.[4] Although the cage crinoline was not meant to be seen, its distinctive skeleton of graduated hoops connected by cloth tapes (p. 93) made an indelible impression on visual culture and is still widely referenced by artists and designers (fig. 10).

Another breakthrough of 1856 was the discovery of synthetic or aniline dyes: eighteen-year-old English chemistry student William Henry Perkin (1838–1907) accidentally invented the world's first effective man-made dye while trying to synthesize quinine. He called the pale purple color *mauve,* the French name for the mallow plant, which has light purple flowers. The new hue received the royal seal of approval when it was adopted by both Empress Eugénie (1826–1920) and Queen Victoria (1819–1901), who wore a mauve dress to her eldest daughter's 1858 wedding.

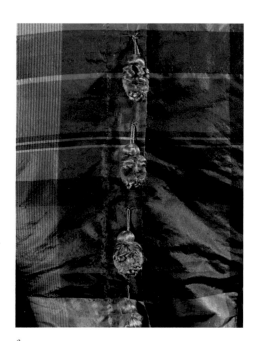

fig. 11
Dress (detail)
France, c. 1855
Page 50

Perkin's discovery led to the synthesis of a veritable rainbow of chemical dyes: mauve was quickly joined by magenta, then yellows, blues, and greens. These aniline dyes could produce vivid shades not found in nature, and they were cheaper to process than dyes made from plants and insects. In contrast to the muted pastels fashionable previously, they were impossible to ignore (fig. 11).

The fashions of the time reflect, and sometimes call attention to, these scientific advances. Early sewing machines could make only long, straight seams; fashion responded by piling on yards and yards of sewn trimmings like ruffles, ribbon, fringe, and braid. The cage crinoline made it possible for skirts to achieve ever-greater circumferences, while innovations in corset construction created an inversely tiny waist. The crinoline also provided an ideal canvas for showing off textiles in the brilliant hues produced by aniline dyes. Women embraced these colors more for their novelty value than for their beauty, and flaunted them with abandon. By 1868 *The Englishwoman's Domestic Magazine* was cautioning readers not to wear more than two of the intense colors at a time, and to tone down the brightest shades with white, black, or gray. Former status symbols like embroidery, cashmere shawls, and tortoiseshell combs fell out of fashion, as these once-exclusive luxuries were now being mass-produced and replicated in cheap, man-made materials. Handmade lace, however, became a sought-after collector's item after inferior machine-made varieties flooded the market.

Women's wardrobes in general expanded to sizes unheard of in previous generations, when even the very wealthy owned relatively few clothes. A woman of fashion might change clothes several times per day, with different dresses for different activities, such as walking, riding, receiving guests, taking tea, dining, and attending the theater. This development was partly a reflection of the new roles and opportunities open to nineteenth-century women, but it would not have been possible without corresponding advances in technology.

Mass production, in addition to changing the course of fashion, had unforeseen social repercussions. Rather than saving professional seamstresses time and energy, the sewing machine simply increased their workload by stimulating the vogue for sewn trimmings; moreover, the most complicated stitching continued to be done by hand. In London seamstresses were so overworked and underpaid that one declared: "No slavery is worse than that of the dressmaker's life."[5] Workers in mechanized textile factories and sweatshops also endured horrific conditions, and many of these workers were children.

The fashions themselves were no less damaging. Tight corsets posed a number of health risks, including fainting, miscarriage, and damage to internal organs. Voluminous dresses trailed on filthy streets and could not be easily washed. Crinolines were apt to fly up in the wind, catch fire, or become entangled in carriage wheels. Queen Victoria herself publicly condemned "the indelicate, expensive, dangerous and hideous article called Crinoline."[6] Some aniline dyes contained traces of arsenic, which irritated the skin and poisoned drinking water near dye works.

There also was growing concern about the moral dangers posed by fashion's artifice and excess. By the mid-nineteenth century, fashion had begun to articulate the tension between progress and nostalgia—between faceless technology and traditional craftsmanship—that unsettled European society.

THE BACKLASH AGAINST MASS PRODUCTION TOOK TWO DIRECTIONS: haute couture and dress reform. Haute couture—literally, "high sewing"—was the term for custom-made fashion, the most exclusive branch of the French fashion industry, which exists to this day. Although those who could afford to had always ordered custom-made clothing, it was now given a special name to distinguish it from ready-to-wear clothing, with its machine stitching and standardized sizing. As part of this symbolic rebranding, the couturier emerged from the workroom and stepped into the spotlight, emblazoning his name on the first clothing labels. These labels, like a painter's signature on a canvas, subtly elevated fashion from trade to art, and the couturier from nameless artisan to celebrity.

fig. 12
Dante Gabriel Rossetti
The Day Dream (Portrait of Jane Morris), 1880
Oil on canvas
Bequeathed by Constantine Alexander, Victoria and
Albert Museum, London

fig. 13
Nathaniel Currier (Currier and Ives, New York)
The Bloomer Costume, 1852
Print/lithograph
Library of Congress

It is fitting that Charles Frederick Worth (1826–1895), the so-called father of haute couture, was an Englishman living in Paris, for haute couture was (and remains) an international affair, headquartered in Paris but attracting customers and couturiers from around the world. For its privileged clientele, haute couture signified quality, individuality, and status in a widening array of clothing choices.

For others, these virtues existed only outside of mainstream fashion. There were several separate but similarly motivated campaigns to reform dress—particularly women's dress—in the late nineteenth century, each with its own agenda and even publications. The English Pre-Raphaelite painters were the first to question the supremacy of modern fashion, dressing their wives and models in loose, flowing dresses and hairstyles inspired by the art of the medieval period (that is, before Raphael, 1483–1520) (fig. 12). In 1851 American feminist Amelia Bloomer (1818–1894) introduced her controversial "Turkish trousers" for women (fig. 13); although her notoriety spread to Europe, the style did not catch on. The Rational Dress Society, formed in London in 1881, promoted healthier and more hygienic dress—including woolen long underwear—for all. England's Royal Society for the Protection of Birds was founded in 1889 in reaction to the popularity of feather-trimmed hats.

One of the most influential groups to address the deficiencies of modern fashion was the aesthetic movement. Unlike other dress-reformers, the aesthetes were not interested in changing contemporary dress. Instead, these progressive artists and intellectuals rejected it entirely, and looked to the past—particularly to antiquity and to the Middle Ages—for an alternative. Modern fashion's chief defect, in the minds of the aesthetes, was that it was simply ugly. The unnatural colors, materials, and silhouettes that emerged from the Industrial Revolution offended taste as much as reason. In the decorative arts as well as in dress, the aesthetes deplored the sameness

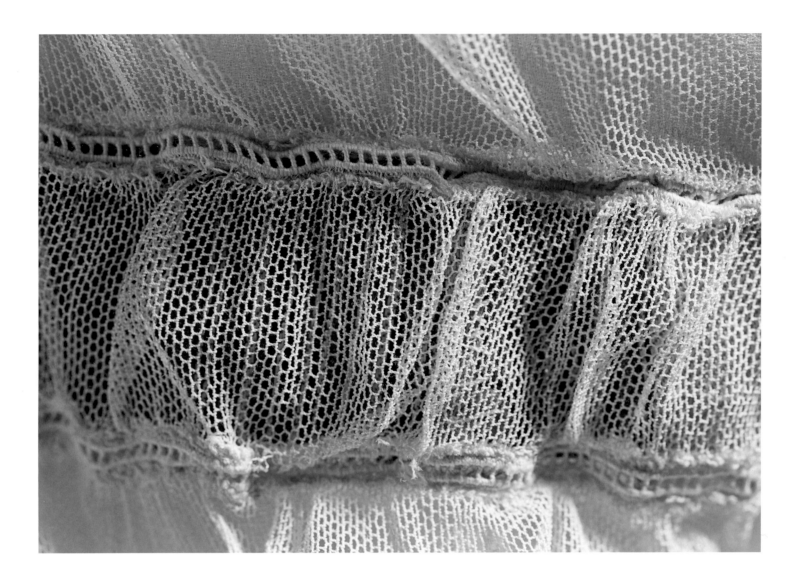

fig. 14
Paul Poiret
Dress (detail), 1909–10
Page 40, right

and poor quality of mass-produced goods. Not content with reviving past styles, they sought to return to old-fashioned methods of clothing production: the use of natural dyes, hand looms, and such hand-worked details as smocking and embroidery. At the same time, they rejected disfiguring emblems of modernity, including corsets, crinolines, and high heels. Although it remained a fringe ideology, the aesthetic movement unwittingly impacted everyday dress. In 1884 the London department store Liberty & Co. opened a costume department that sold "artistic dress," a mainstream distillation of aesthetic dress (p. 112).

Couturiers also participated in the mania for fashion revivals. Worth made historicism his signature, studying Renaissance and seventeenth-century portraits and copying elements of the subjects' dress, such as lace collars, ribbon rosettes, and voluminous sleeves. Other couturiers followed Worth's profitable example. The "Louis" revival of the late 1800s, referring to Kings Louis XV (1710–1774) and XVI (1754–1793), looked back to the eighteenth century, with its square necklines, elbow-length sleeves, and draped overskirts. Couturier Jacques Doucet (1853–1929) assembled a vast collection of eighteenth-century French art, which informed his delicate designs. The leg-of-mutton sleeve of the 1890s was a revival of a style originally seen in the 1830s that had been inflated by down-filled sleeve plumpers (p. 87 left). A surviving dress with leg-of-mutton sleeves by the Rouff couture house also has Renaissance touches: lush velvet trimmings and spiky ruffles at the collar and cuffs (pp. 10, 113). As Europe's elite segregated itself into old and new money, owning a dress based on an Old Master painting lent a woman considerable cultural and intellectual cachet—almost as much as owning the painting itself.

fig. 15
Paul Iribe
Plate from *Les Robes de Paul Poiret*, 1908
Wood engraving with *pochoir* and hand-coloring
(watercolor) on paper
Doris Stein Research Center, LACMA

Perhaps it was centennial malaise that drove designers to look backward, rather than forward, as the nineteenth century turned into the twentieth. A hundred years after its first appearance, the neoclassical, or Empire, line was revived by couturiers Paul Poiret (1879–1944), Mariano Fortuny (1871–1949), and Madeleine Vionnet (1876–1975)—considered some of the most innovative designers of their generation. The pared-down white sheath of tissue-thin silk net that Poiret made for his wife, Denise, in 1909 was extremely avant-garde for its time but actually looked back a hundred years to Empress Josephine's day. Strips of a colorful striped silk twill are encased between two layers of net (fig. 14); the uppermost strip suggests the Empire waistline (p. 40 right). Just as the original Empire style had followed a period of excessive trimmings and disfiguring hoops and corsets, the twentieth-century Empire revival was largely a reaction against fashions that its creators considered abominable, such as S-curve corsets, leg-of-mutton sleeves, and *froufrou*, a French term meaning a rustling sound that was applied to the fussy frills of Belle Epoque fashion. Poiret gave his dresses names like Directoire and Joséphine, confirming that the Empire revival of the early 1900s was born of nostalgia for the early 1800s, not for ancient Greece and Rome (fig. 15). As fashion revivals multiplied and repeated in the nineteenth century, it frequently was difficult to tell whether the revival commemorated the original fashion or a subsequent revival.

As in the eighteenth century, art was the lens through which these progressive designers and thinkers connected with temporally (and often geographically) distant cultures. Both forward-thinking couturiers and antifashion aesthetes could agree that "the best way to decide on a really beautiful dress is by studying the pictures of the great masters of light and shade, and copying them," as dress reformer Mary Haweis (1848–1898) wrote in 1878.[7] The emerging field of the study of dress history provided a steady supply of illustrated books on the history of world dress that were avidly read by artists, scholars, couturiers, and connoisseurs, as well as by masquerade and theater costume designers.

THESE TECHNICAL AND STYLISTIC ADVANCES (and strategic stylistic retreats) were largely confined to women's dress. After the French Revolution, menswear took a sober, austere new direction, from which it never fully rebounded. Men had always possessed fewer clothes than women, but those clothes had been equally colorful and ornate. In fact, during the eighteenth century, lace, embroidery, sequins, fur, ribbons, muffs, and high heels were considered unisex ornaments. The Revolution redefined masculinity, stripping it of all such markers of status, wealth, and individuality. As pioneering artist and designer William Morris (1834–1896) put it in 1894: "Civilisation has settled for us males that art shall have no place in our clothes."[8]

The three-piece suit continued to be the male uniform, but it was now worn with trousers, not breeches. Historically, trousers were a working garment, the dress of the lower-class *sans-culottes* (literally, "without breeches"), who instigated the French Revolution. Although men's fashions did not change as quickly or as dramatically as women's, subtle changes in cut and construction marked the evolution of taste. The neoclassical aesthetic of the early nineteenth century dictated body-conscious styles in imitation of ancient nude (or near-nude) statues. Close-fitting tailcoats and morning coats exposed the full expanse of legs clad in tight pantaloons (p. 43 right). By the 1830s, these revealing garments were reserved for formal and evening wear; by day, men wore fuller trousers and long, skirted frock coats (fig. 16). These skirts widened and waists narrowed in sympathy with the fashionable female silhouette. And men employed a variety of artificial means—from shoulder and chest pads to waist binders—to achieve the ideal proportions (pp. 90–91). Beginning in the 1860s, the lounge jacket, a relatively loose garment without a waist seam, similar to the modern suit jacket, offered a casual alternative to the frock coat, which was increasingly relegated to formal occasions.

One of the rare constants in the history of fashion is that the casual wear of one generation inevitably becomes the formal wear of the next, a fate bemoaned by *The Tailor and Cutter* magazine in 1878: "We are rapidly degenerating into a slipshod

fig. 17
Jean Paul Gaultier
Paris Fashion Week, Winter 1996–97 Menswear

fig. 16 (opposite)
Coat
France, 1816–20
Page 43

fig. 18
Christopher Bailey for Burberry Prorsum, *Milan Fashion Week, Autumn/Winter 2009–2010 Menswear on 17 January 2009*

state of things. After a time Frock coats and even Morning coats will be entirely a thing of the past and if things continue on in this way will only be seen at museums where they will serve to amuse a wondering and awestricken group of sight-seers." History has proven the truth of that prediction, although menswear designers periodically revive the romantic suit styles of the past, complete with hats, cravats, and other antiquated accessories (figs. 16–18).

Regardless of their cut, by the second half of the nineteenth century, these suits were almost always black, brown, or gray. It was an appropriate uniform for the new Europe: no longer feudal and agricultural, instead middle class and industrial. The plain, dark suit was the mark of the businessman, not the leisured aristocrat. Timeless, simple, and respectable, it served as a social leveler, erasing economic and regional distinctions. Expressions of personality were pushed to the periphery— eccentric facial hair, elaborately knotted cravats, and vibrant patterned vests (fig. 19)—or confined to the privacy of the home, where men could relax in outlandish dressing gowns, caps, slippers (p. 153), and smoking accessories. Color, embroidery, and other embellishments appeared only on court costume and military dress uniforms. Skilled tailoring and quietly luxurious textiles, rather than ostentatious trimmings, distinguished the man of substance and taste (fig. 20).

fig. 19
Vest (detail)
England, c. 1840
Page 61

fig. 20
Coat (detail)
Probably England, 1825–30
Page 43

Naturally, there were exceptions to this rule, and alternative fashions flourished outside the mainstream. The dandy of the teens and twenties affected simplicity in his dress, but lavished money and attention on meticulous tailoring and grooming. He was resurrected as the midcentury flaneur, the idle man-about-town whose carefully cultivated elegance incorporated bohemian flourishes. The aesthetes—led by Oscar Wilde (1854–1900), who declared fashion to be "a form of ugliness so intolerable that we have to alter it every six months"—advocated a wholesale return to the picturesque luxuries of times past, wearing velvet jackets, flowing ties, long hair, and breeches.[9] And even the most conventional businessmen donned comfortable, casual sportswear for golfing, hunting, and yachting.

Modern science did manage to impact menswear in its tailoring practices. Recognized as a British specialty—Savile Row in London was the physical and spiritual center of the trade—men's tailoring was an art form, passed down through generations of skilled craftsmen. In the mid-nineteenth century, new, scientific methods of measurement and sizing helped custom or "bespoke" tailors throughout Europe achieve a more perfect fit for their clients, while standardization of ready-to-wear sizes put Savile Row within reach of Main Street. In the eighteenth century, colorful, luxurious textiles and trimmings often had disguised imprecise tailoring; now that menswear was pared down to a blank slate, a perfect fit was the measure of a man's fashionability.

As menswear faded into black, the female body was—more than ever—the site of luxury, display, creativity, and color. Economist Thorstein Veblen (1857–1929) in his 1899 book *The Theory of the Leisure Class* identified the wife as the "ceremonial consumer" of her husband's goods: her clothing expressed her husband's professional, financial, and social success in a way that his own tastefully restrained attire could not.[10] Veblen coined the term "conspicuous consumption" to describe the acquisition of goods for the purpose of advertising one's wealth and establishing one's social status. In public, a gentleman was, by definition, inconspicuous. But his wife and daughters wore his reputation on their backs.

fig. 21
James Abbott McNeill Whistler
The Princess from the Land of Porcelain (La Princesse du pays de la porcelaine), 1863–65
Oil on canvas
Gift of Charles Lang Freer, Freer Gallery of Art and Arthur M. Sackler Gallery, Smithsonian Institution

fig. 22
John Galliano for Christian Dior, *Paris Haute Couture Week, Angela Lindvall wearing kimono, Spring/Summer 2007*

fig. 23
Dressing Gown (detail)
Japan for the Western market, c. 1885
Page 146

AS THE NINETEENTH CENTURY TURNED INTO THE TWENTIETH, the bonds between art and fashion grew stronger and more deeply entwined. The term *Japonisme* was coined in 1872 to describe the Western fascination with Japanese art and design, which played a key role in the development of the impressionist, aesthetic, and art nouveau movements, as well as permeating fashion and popular culture. In 1854 Japan—largely cut off from the West since the early 1600s—opened its ports to foreign trade. By the 1870s, Japanese fabrics and kimonos (as well as prints, curios, and decorative arts) were ubiquitous in Europe, thanks in part to international expositions attended by large Japanese delegations (figs. 21, 23). In 1880 the *Gazette des Beaux-Arts* reported "an epidemic of fans," many of them imported from Japan or imitating Japanese fans.[11] Small, inexpensive accessories like shawls and fans had expanded the Asian trade to include Europe's growing middle-class market. These customers did not have the means (or the social confidence) to wear garments *à l'Orient* from head to toe, but they still wanted to add discreetly exotic touches to their wardrobes and homes. Asian exports served as status symbols on many levels, testifying to the wearer's wealth, fashionability, erudition, and connoisseurship of Japanese art. European interpretations of Asian dress, vague and whimsical in the eighteenth century, became more accurate and specific, and Western fashion's fascination with Japan continues to this day (fig. 22).

In the first decade of the twentieth century, groundbreaking young men—and, increasingly, women—produced fashions in geometric patterns and bold primary colors inspired by cubist art, which was in turn heavily influenced by African art. They borrowed forms, motifs, and textiles from other cultures as well, introducing unstructured garments like tunics, caftans, capes, and cocoon coats (p. 62) inspired by the dress of Japan, China, Egypt, India, the Middle East, and the Americas. These designs appeared both primitive and audaciously modern when compared to the anodyne pastels, disfiguring corsets, and frothy ruffles and laces of the Belle Epoque. A few even dared to dress European women in loose trousers, succeeding where Amelia Bloomer had failed a half-century earlier by calling them "lounging pajamas" and camouflaging their controversial feminism with exotic "Oriental" accessories: turbans, veils, and feathers (pp. 176–177).

Whether in art or in fashion, this global awareness and integration had a common purpose beyond mere shock value. Fashion is, by definition, ephemeral. What comes into fashion must go out of fashion, if only until it enjoys a revival. The major European art movements of the late nineteenth and early twentieth centuries—including art nouveau in France, the Wiener Werkstätte style in Austria, and the arts and crafts movement, centered in England—aimed to encompass all nations and all forms of the visual arts, from painting to fashion to furniture. For the first time in history, architects designed dresses, painters created textiles, and couturiers decorated interiors. Art and fashion, East and West, old and new united to produce objects that combined beauty and functionality.

These idealistic artists and designers hoped that by drawing inspiration from all over the world and from all epochs of history, fashion would become truly international and timeless. Fashion would cheat death.

Timeline

Fashioning Fashion: European Dress in Detail, 1700–1915 is organized around the physical processes of creating fashionable garments. In the context of eighteenth- and nineteenth-century Europe, these processes can be broken down into four key stages: First, the creator draws inspiration from the tastes and trends of his or her era. Next, a two-dimensional textile is selected. This textile may be a work of art in its own right, but it is not the finished product. It has to be tailored—that is, cut and sewn. Finally, the tailored garment is embellished with trimmings, whether simple fastenings or intricate and costly ornamentation.

Historically, the textile, tailoring, and trimming techniques represented in *Fashioning Fashion* were regarded as art forms, passed down through professional guilds and generations of skilled artisans. Today, many of them are found only in haute couture, the exclusive Parisian fashion houses that create custom-made, hand-finished garments for private clients. Most clothes—and the materials used to make them—are produced quickly and cheaply using machines; computers have simplified the tailoring process. This makes fashion available to a much wider audience, but at the expense of the quality and individuality evident in the garments found in *Fashioning Fashion*.

This opening section, Timeline, is the only part of *Fashioning Fashion* that is presented chronologically, rather than by theme or technique. It charts the major changes that took place in the female and male silhouettes from 1700 to 1915. A garment's silhouette serves as an important indicator of its origins. Formal properties—such as the shape of a sleeve, the height of a hemline, and the relative proportions of the chest, waist, and hips (often achieved by padding or cinching)—combine to anchor a garment in its time and place.

In order to call attention to the silhouette, the women's garments in this section are predominantly white. Though white has enjoyed varying degrees of popularity and symbolic significance in different epochs and cultures, it has not fallen out of fashion since the late eighteenth century. It is often credited with being flattering to women of all ages and complexions, and, in the periods covered in this publication when clothes could not be washed easily, it was a conspicuous status symbol. Because of its traditional association with purity, white has been worn by European brides since the eighteenth century; however, not one of these gowns is known to be a wedding dress. From the ballroom to the garden, they were worn for occasions as diverse as their shapes.

Although the changes in the male silhouette were not as frequent or dramatic, menswear was far from dull. Indeed, in the eighteenth century, men dressed as colorfully and ornately as women; however, after the French Revolution, eye-catching colors and trimmings were increasingly relegated to leisure wear, sportswear, and military uniform. Thereafter, fashionable men displayed their taste and wealth through innovative tailoring and flamboyant accessories. But there have always been exceptions: iconoclastic individuals who were not afraid to be labeled dandies.

By 1915 both women and men had begun to shed their cumbersome layers and body-altering undergarments. As the century progressed, androgyny in dress more and more became the hallmark of modernity.

1765

For most of the eighteenth century, women had two fashion choices: the French-style gown (*robe à la française*) and the form-fitting English-style gown (*robe à l'anglaise*). Although named for their countries of origin, both styles were worn simultaneously throughout Europe. This *robe à la française* is shaped to fit the wide, rectangular hoop petticoat worn at the English court.

DRESS (ROBE À LA FRANÇAISE)
England, c. 1765
Silk satin with weft-float patterning and silk passementerie
Gift of Mrs. Henry Salvatori, M.79.19.1

STOMACHER
Europe, 1725–75
Silk satin with metallic-thread embroidery
M.2007.211.132

1780–1790

With the revival in the 1780s of interest in classical antiquity—and the simultaneous proliferation of washable cotton fabrics—white became highly fashionable for women. This *robe à l'anglaise* embroidered in a delicate floral pattern exemplifies the simplicity of the neoclassical style.

DRESS (ROBE À L'ANGLAISE)
England, 1780–90
Cotton plain weave with wool embroidery
Costume Council Fund, M.59.25A

HAT
Italy, c. 1780
Straw with silk plain-weave trim
Gift of Miss May Routh, M.83.162.4

FICHU
France, c. 1780
Cotton plain weave (muslin) with silk embroidery
M.2007.211.143

1800

The French Revolution revived the fashions and hairstyles of ancient Greece and Rome, transforming the female silhouette. The so-called "neoclassical" look reflected a larger cultural interest in the democratic politics and philosophies of those civilizations. Under Napoléon, the silhouette became known as the Empire style. Thin white muslin sheaths with low necklines, short sleeves, and high waistlines left little to the imagination. Shawls from India provided warmth and visual interest, while echoing the flowing drapery of ancient statues.

DRESS
Probably India for the Western market, c. 1800
Cotton plain weave (muslin) with silk embroidery
M.2007.211.867

SHAWL
Kashmir, India, c. 1810
Goat-fleece underdown (cashmere wool) twill with double-interlocking tapestry-weave patterning
Mr. and Mrs. Allan C. Balch Collection, M.45.3.150

1825

During the Romantic era, sleeves began to widen, waistlines dropped slightly, and skirts flared out at the hem. The fashionable hourglass silhouette was enhanced by details on the upper and lower areas of dresses. Here, the satin panelike trim on the sleeves and the undulating tubular trim (*rouleau*) on the skirt emphasize volume while the transparent fabric gives the impression of a delicate lightness.

DRESS
Europe, c. 1825
Silk net with silk embroidery and silk satin trim
M.2007.211.935

PAIR OF SHOES
Europe, 1825–50
Silk satin and leather
M.2007.211.324A–B

1830

The exaggerated silhouette of this Romantic-era dress was achieved with extremely voluminous leg-of-mutton or *gigot* sleeves—full at the upper arm and fitted at the forearm—that create a shoulder width equal in size to the skirt's flounced hemline.

DRESS
England, c. 1830
Cotton plain weave with cotton cutwork embroidery (*broderie anglaise*)

M.2007.211.740

PAIR OF SHOES
England, 1825–50
Silk satin and leather

M.2007.211.312A–B

1845–1849

By the mid-1840s, dresses with sloped shoulders, tight bodices with fitted sleeves, and fuller skirts mirrored the similarly constricting social norms of the early Victorian woman. Bodices often included rows of pleats extending over the shoulder to the waist in a pronounced V-shape that pointed to the wide, cartridge-pleated skirt (p. 34).

DRESS
England, 1845–49
Silk plain weave with warp-float patterning, printed, silk lace and silk passementerie

M.2007.211.744

BONNET
England, c. 1845
Straw with silk-ribbon trim

M.2007.211.168

1855

Lightweight cage crinolines were introduced in 1856, replacing the multiple layers of petticoats previously needed to support the shape of wide, full skirts. As a result, dome-shaped skirts grew to massive proportions, with tiered flounces increasing the volume.

DRESS
Europe, c. 1855
Cotton plain weave (muslin) with cotton embroidery
M.2007.211.755

1885

From the late 1860s, skirt volume shifted to the posterior. This day dress illustrates the extreme bustle silhouette popular by the 1880s, which was characterized by a protruding shelf-like fullness to the back. By necessity, these dresses were constructed with a separate bodice and skirt.

DRESS
Europe, 1885
Cotton plain weave with cotton cutwork embroidery (*broderie anglaise*) and cotton needle lace
M.2007.211.850A–B

PAIR OF SHOES
Europe, c. 1885
Leather
Gift of Mrs. Margaret Hubbard Taber, M.86.410.2A–B

1908

By the turn of the twentieth century, the bustle had radically decreased in amplitude. The new silhouette constricted the abdomen, thrust the breast forward, and forced the shoulders and the derriere back into a well-defined serpentine curve, which in profile resembled the letter S. This dress's sinuous outline and linear patterns highlighted with cording exemplify the fluid dynamism of the international style of art nouveau (p. 13).

DRESS
Europe, c. 1908
Cotton crepe and cotton net with cotton embroidery
M.2007.211.791

1909–1910

Reminiscent of the radical change in silhouette that had occurred a century before, the early twentieth century witnessed a transition from the hourglass to the cylinder. Typical of vanguard designer Paul Poiret's revival of the Empire style, this columnar, gracefully flowing dress illustrates the diminished role of the corset. Its simplicity is belied by hand-worked channels of diaphanous fabric over strips of silk twill (p. 26), which reflect the popularity of drawn-thread work and the gossamer lightness of lingerie.

Paul Poiret
France, 1879–1944

DRESS, 1909–10
Silk net, silk plain weave, and silk twill
M.2007.211.945

1755

The three-piece suit emerged in the late seventeenth century and quickly established itself as a male uniform for the ages. Originally, the suit consisted of a coat, long-sleeved waistcoat, and breeches. By the 1740s, however, sleeveless waistcoats were more common. Here, false waistcoat cuffs protruding from the coat's sleeves create the illusion that more of the richly textured velvet has been used.

SUIT
France, c. 1755
Silk cut, uncut, and voided velvet (*ciselé*) on satin foundation
M.2007.211.947A–C

1765

In the mid-eighteenth century, the fronts of men's coats began to expose the waistcoat, as seen in this example. Although highly decorative, none of the silver-thread embroidered buttons on the coat are functional; three sets of hook and eyes fasten it at midchest. As the eighteenth century progressed, the sleeves and skirts of coats became narrower, waistcoats shorter, and breeches tighter, creating a streamlined male silhouette.

SUIT
France, c. 1765
Silk plain weave (faille) with metallic-thread passementerie
M.2007.211.41A–C

1785

This wool three-piece suit illustrates the nascent influence of English sportswear on European fashions. Wool fabric, plain buttons, and the absence of trim reference the simplicity and practicality of suits worn in the English countryside.

SUIT
Spain, c. 1785
Wool plain weave, full finish, with silk cut velvet on twill foundation
M.2007.211.801A–C

HAT (TRICORNE)
Europe or United States, c. 1780
Beaver fur
Mrs. Alice F. Schott Bequest, M.67.8.204

1790–1795

The French Revolution made fashion and luxury synonymous with tyranny and treason. However, some fierce opponents of the Revolution expressed their views by dressing with conspicuous elegance, wearing colorful silks and lace and breeches (*culottes*) instead of politically correct, working-class trousers. Men on both sides of the political divide carried twisted sticks, "Hercules clubs," to defend themselves against partisan attacks.

COAT
France, c. 1785, altered c. 1795
Silk plain weave and silk satin stripes
M.2007.211.805

VEST
France, c. 1790
Silk satin and silk cut velvet with printed warp on satin foundation stripes
Gift of Dr. and Mrs. Pratapaditya Pal, AC1995.253.1

BREECHES
France, c. 1790
Silk plain-weave stripes
M.2007.211.1077

WALKING STICK
France, 1790–95
Wood
M.2007.211.831

1816–1820

The frock coat of the nineteenth century—characterized by a fitted torso buttoned to the waist, straight-cut front edges, and full skirt attached by a waist seam (p. 28)—probably was inspired by the greatcoats worn by soldiers in the Napoleonic wars. In contrast to this colorful example, the frock coat grew shorter, plainer, and more formal throughout the century.

COAT
France, 1816–20
Silk and wool twill
Purchased with funds provided by Michael and
Ellen Michelson, M.2010.33.7

TROUSERS
Europe, c. 1830–45
Cotton twill with cut supplementary weft floats (corduroy)
M.2007.211.706

TOP HAT
Boston, Massachusetts, c. 1832
Beaver Fur
Costume Council Curatorial Discretionary Fund, M.87.209.2

1825–1830

During the first half of the nineteenth century, the typical male ensemble included a somber tailcoat, colorful vest, and trousers. The tailcoat, cut to the waist at the front and tapered into long tails at the back, was informed by English riding coats. In the early part of the century, lightweight silk-crepe pantaloons exhibited the natural lines of the lower body, emulating the ancient Greek and Roman nude statues that influenced neoclassical fashion of the period.

COAT
Probably England, 1825–30
Wool plain weave, full finish, with silk cut velvet on twill foundation
Costume Council Curatorial Discretionary Fund, AC1993.127.1

PANTALOONS
Scotland, 1825–50
Silk crepe
M.2007.211.1076

STOCK
Boston, Massachusetts, c. 1830
Silk satin
Gift of Mrs. Lawrence R. Tollenaere in memory of her mother, Marie Adeline Huber Hansen, AC1998.78.1

TOP HAT
Paris, c. 1815
Beaver fur
M.2007.211.827

1840–1845

By 1840 the thigh-length frock coat was worn for both formal and informal dress. This single-breasted coat and loose-fitting trousers of lightweight patterned fabrics probably were worn for recreational wear in the country.

COAT
Europe, c. 1845
Cotton plain weave with supplementary warp-float patterning
M.2007.211.61

TROUSERS
France, 1840
Cotton and silk twill
M.2007.211.707

STOCK
England, c. 1840
Silk plain weave
Mrs. Alice F. Schott Bequest, CR.448.67–74

TOP HAT
New York City, c. 1840–60
Beaver fur
Costume Council Fund, AC1992.7.1

1875–1880

An informal alternative to the frock coat, the short lounge jacket introduced around 1855 had no waist seam, skirt, or tails. Its loose fit was comfortable and did not require custom tailoring; in England it generally was worn with a bowler (originally designed for riding horses) instead of a top hat. This transitional style retains the waist seam and vent in back; however, the flamboyant tartan defies the growing uniformity of men's fashion.

SUIT
England, 1875–80
Wool twill
Purchased with funds provided by Michael and
Ellen Michelson, M.2010.33.9A–B

HAT (BOWLER)
United States, c. 1875–1900
Wool felt
Gift of Mrs. Fredric H. Sturdy, CR.74.13.2

1880

In the late eighteenth and early nineteenth centuries, a gentleman started his day by riding or hunting. The morning coat was designed for comfort on horseback. Although similar in cut and function to the tailcoat, the morning coat is usually identified by front edges that slope back in a curve, rather than a horizontal line. The style was adopted for everyday use, as in this example; it is still worn as formal daywear.

COAT AND VEST
England, c. 1880
Wool twill with wool braid trim
Purchased with funds provided
by Michael and Ellen Michelson,
M.2010.33.15A–B

TOP HAT
Boston, United States, c. 1870
Beaver fur
M.2007.211.453

NECKTIE
France, 1890–1910
Silk twill and plain weave with
supplementary weft patterning
Purchased with funds provided
by Michael and Ellen Michelson,
M.2010.33.27

1911

The gray, pinstriped, made-to-measure lounge suit was the uniform of the Edwardian businessman, and it has remained a menswear staple ever since, with only slight changes in cut. Its numerous pockets made it as practical as it was comfortable. There are four in this vest, three in the trousers, and five in the jacket, one of them containing the tailor's label inscribed with the date and the name of the owner, "D. R. Home Esq."

SUIT
London, 1911
Wool twill
Purchased with funds provided by Michael and
Ellen Michelson, M.2010.33.11A–C

WALKING CANE
Europe, c. 1900
Wood, ivory, lizard skin, and brass
Gift of Pasadena Art Museum, CR.265.63–150

HAT (BOWLER)
United States, c. 1915
Wool felt
Gift of Mrs. Carl W. Barrow, M.88.40.2

Textiles

There are fashions in textiles as well as in clothing. Each garment in this section is a fine example of the latest silhouette and tailoring and trimming techniques of its time, yet the first thing that catches the eye is the extraordinary textile.

The marriage of warp and weft has produced an infinite variety of patterns and textures, from the plain weave—a simple over-and-under interlacing—to intricate figured silks and velvets. In addition to woven effects, patterns and textures could be applied to textiles through heating, glazing, painting, pressing, or printing with blocks or rollers. Dyes—whether natural or, from 1856, synthetic—played a transformative role in the manufacturing process.

The eighteenth and nineteenth centuries saw the rapid mechanization and industrialization of spinning and weaving, and a corresponding increase in the amount of fabric a single weaver could produce in a given amount of time. Rather than being welcomed, these innovations created controversy, as they put countless skilled workers out of a job. However, new technologies did help make new clothing widely available and affordable, and brought fashion within reach of the swiftly expanding European middle class.

Before the first man-made fiber, artificial silk, was patented in 1892, textiles for clothing used four principal plant and animal fibers: wool, silk, cotton, and linen (the latter primarily in undergarments). Through careful manipulation and blending of these fibers, manufacturers could produce hundreds of distinct textiles, from woolens so dense they were effectively waterproof to transparent gauzes.

In eighteenth-century high fashion, textiles and clothing were two distinct industries: a customer bought a length of fabric from a mercer, then took it to a tailor or dressmaker to have it sewn into a garment. The cloth cost much more than the tailoring, for textiles represented a significant investment of time, labor, and resources. By the second half of the nineteenth century, clothing production and distribution were streamlined by mechanization and the establishment of department stores, but fabric continued to be made of costly natural materials.

Silk was the most expensive and prestigious fiber, particularly when woven into complex figured textiles. From the late seventeenth century, Europe's silk-production centers issued new designs on a regular and predictable basis, with seasonal offerings appearing every six months. A fashionable pattern or color would be hopelessly outdated within a year. This emphasis on novelty ensured the industry's prosperity in the face of competition from foreign imports, including silks from China and cashmeres and printed cottons from India.

Historic textiles are notoriously fragile, vulnerable to light, pests, and fluctuations in temperature. Many have been damaged by chemicals in dyes, cleaning products, and the environment. Due to the high cost of textiles in the eighteenth and nineteenth centuries, it was common practice to use and reuse them until they wore out. Yet, through chance or someone's particular care, these examples have survived to tell the story of evolving tastes and technologies.

In weaving, a single throw of the shuttle that carries a bobbin of weft thread is called a "shot." So-called "shot silk" is a fabric created when the vertical warp and horizontal weft differ in color. Known in French as *changeant* (changeable) silk, it changes colors when seen in varying angles and under different lighting conditions. Although this suit appears purple like its warp, it has a green weft; together these produce a rich iridescent sheen characteristic of shot silk.

SUIT
Europe, c. 1790, altered c. 1805
Coat and breeches: silk plain weave (shot taffeta) with sequins and metallic-thread embroidery; waistcoat: silk satin with sequins and metallic-thread embroidery
M.2007.211.800A–C

SHIRT RUFFLE
Europe, c. 1800
Linen plain weave
M.2007.211.976

Even with the most basic textile structure like plain weave, infinite plaid patterns are possible through the arrangement of colors in both the vertical warp and horizontal weft. The silk taffeta plaid of this elegant dress evokes traditional wool twill tartans worn by the Highlanders of Scotland. Tartans crossed over from regional dress into high fashion when Queen Victoria built her Highland retreat, Balmoral Castle, in 1853, instigating a trend for all things Scottish.

DRESS
France, c. 1855
Silk plain weave (taffeta)
M.2007.211.767

In the second half of the
eighteenth century, France
was a leader in producing
warp resist-dyed silks (*chiné à
la branche*) inspired by central
Asian ikats (textiles in which
the warp and/or weft yarns
have been resist-dyed before
weaving). The characteristic
hazy, impressionistic patterns
were popular for dress and
upholstery. By 1837 a mechanical
process of roller-printing warps
(shadow printing) created
textiles simulating *chiné à la
branche* but with the capability
of creating realistic pictorial
patterns, such as the Japanese-
inspired butterfly-and-flower
motif on this two-piece dress.
The blurriness of the design is
underscored by the watery effect
of the moiré finish (p. 46).

DRESS
France, c. 1865
Silk plain weave (taffeta) with printed
warp, moiré finish
M.2007.211.943B–C

When viewed from afar, this dress appears to be made from popular lightweight plain-weave muslin; however, upon closer examination, gauze—a loosely woven open-mesh fabric created when two or more vertical warp elements are twisted around each other and locked in place by the insertion of a horizontal weft element—is identified. A complementary bobbin-net flounce ruffle draws attention down toward the hem, where a stylized neoclassical pattern embroidered in wool reinforces the ancient inspiration for this garment.

DRESS
France, c. 1820
Cotton gauze and cotton bobbin net with wool embroidery and silk satin trim
M.2007.211.18

Long shawls produced in Kashmir, India, of the finest goat-fleece underdown became fashionable accessories worn with the diaphanous neoclassical dresses of the late eighteenth and early nineteenth centuries. Woven in twill—a weave structure in which one set of warps and wefts passes over two or more elements and under one or more elements of the opposing set to form floats in a diagonal alignment—Kashmir shawls often had decorative borders of stylized flowers or shrubs with bending tips (*buta*).

SHAWL
Kashmir, India, c. 1800
Goat-fleece underdown (cashmere wool) interlocking twill tapestry weave
From the Nasli and Alice Heeramaneck Collection, Museum Associates Purchase
M.71.1.39

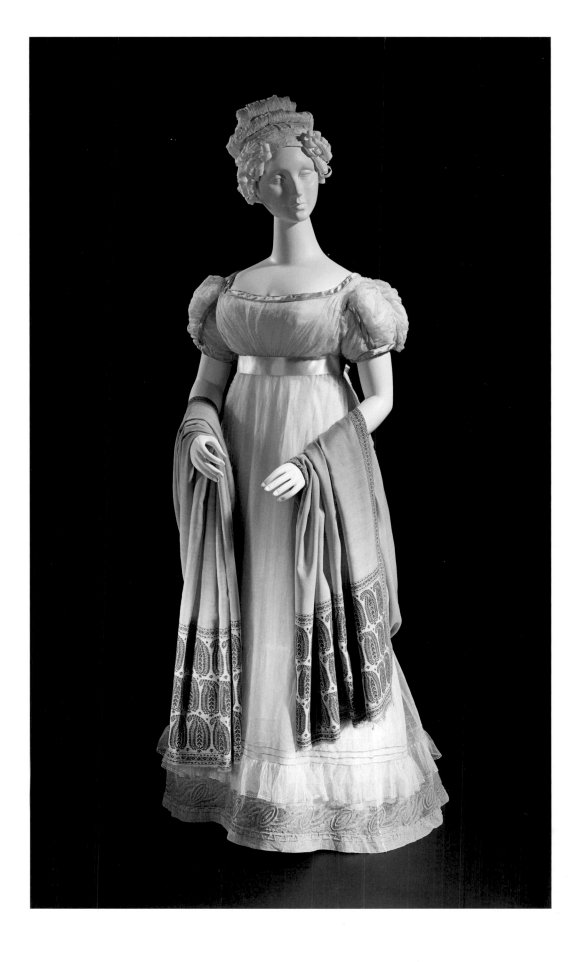

From the end of the seventeenth century through the first quarter of the eighteenth century, figured silks with bold asymmetrical patterns that combined realistic and imagined motifs emerged from the looms of London, Lyon, and Venice. Inspired by the influx of imported Asian textiles, these "bizarre silks" were utilized for both furnishings and fashionable dress, such as this sleeved waistcoat with a curious tiered motif resembling an exotic plant or a stylized pagoda.

WAISTCOAT
France, c. 1715
Silk satin with supplementary weft patterning bound in twill (lampas)
M.2007.211.40

The large meandering floral
pattern, with details that appear
to mimic lace, found on this coat
was woven in a technique known
as lampas—the white pattern
comprises a supplementary warp
and weft bound in plain weave;
the foundation weave consists of
a brown warp and weft. Though
similar to "lace-patterned"
silks popular from 1715 to 1730,
this design is more fluid and
naturalistic.

COAT
France, 1745–50
Silk plain weave with supplementary
weft patterning bound in plain weave
(lampas)
M.2007.211.795

Repeating patterns of fanciful
vignettes depicting whimsical
human figures, fantastic
architectural structures, and
out-of-scale flora and fauna
appear on this figured silk
fashioned into a dress. Typical of
eighteenth-century chinoiserie
designs, this textile illustrates
how Westerners imagined the
exotic Far East. The design,
fabric structure, and thirty-and-
one-half-inch selvage-to-selvage
width are consistent with textiles
produced in Amsterdam during
the first half of the eighteenth
century.

DRESS (ROBE À LA FRANÇAISE)
Amsterdam, 1740–60
Silk satin with silk and metallic-thread
supplementary weft-float patterning
M.2007.211.928

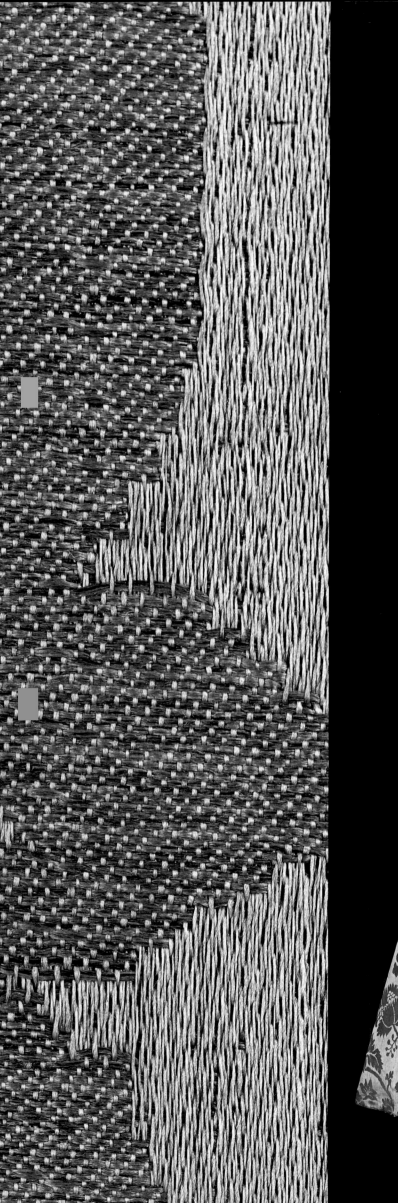

This monochrome figured silk with a pattern woven in satin on a plain-weave foundation *(damassé)* is a variant form of classic satin damask—a reversible-patterned cloth in which the contrast between the front and reverse side of a satin weave is shown on one surface. Produced in China, this patterned silk was made into a fashionable banyan, a garment influenced by East Asian and Persian robes.

MAN'S AT-HOME ROBE (BANYAN)
Textile: China, 1700–1750; robe:
the Netherlands, 1750–60
Silk satin and silk plain weave
(damassé)
M.2007.211.797

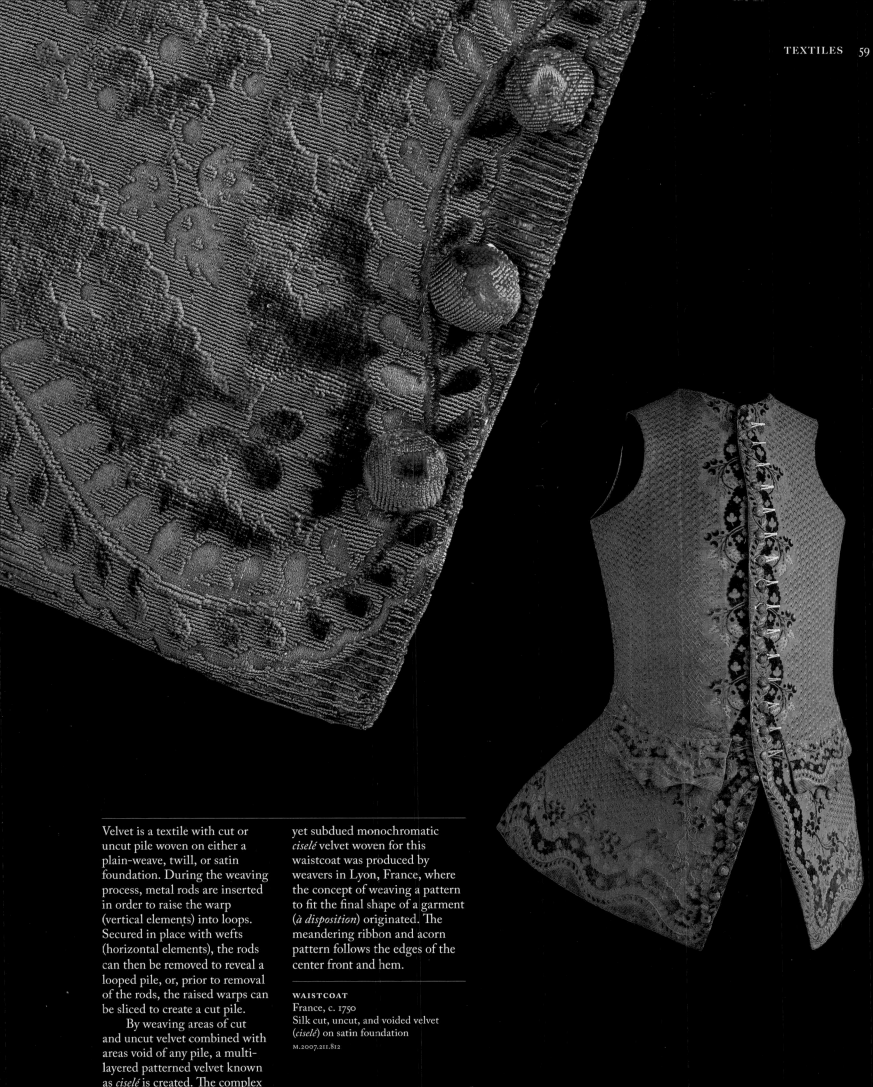

Velvet is a textile with cut or uncut pile woven on either a plain-weave, twill, or satin foundation. During the weaving process, metal rods are inserted in order to raise the warp (vertical elements) into loops. Secured in place with wefts (horizontal elements), the rods can then be removed to reveal a looped pile, or, prior to removal of the rods, the raised warps can be sliced to create a cut pile.

By weaving areas of cut and uncut velvet combined with areas void of any pile, a multi-layered patterned velvet known as *ciselé* is created. The complex yet subdued monochromatic *ciselé* velvet woven for this waistcoat was produced by weavers in Lyon, France, where the concept of weaving a pattern to fit the final shape of a garment (*à disposition*) originated. The meandering ribbon and acorn pattern follows the edges of the center front and hem.

WAISTCOAT
France, c. 1750
Silk cut, uncut, and voided velvet (*ciselé*) on satin foundation
M.2007.211.812

A wide variety of patterned velvets were utilized on nineteenth-century vests, adding color, texture, and sheen to the increasingly somber and lusterless fashionable men's suit. Vests were sartorial vehicles for personal expression and identity.

VEST
England, c. 1855
Silk cut and voided velvet on satin foundation with supplementary weft-float patterning
M.2007.211.821

VEST
England, c. 1850
Silk cut and voided velvet on twill foundation with supplementary weft-float patterning
M.2007.211.820

VEST
England, c. 1845
Silk cut and uncut velvet on twill
foundation
M.2007.211.819

VEST
England, c. 1840
Silk cut and voided velvet on plain-
weave foundation with supplementary
weft-float twill patterning
M.2007.211.818

Gold-metallic thread is woven throughout the foundation of this luxurious velvet; however, its presence is indiscernible to the naked eye except in the limited voided-velvet areas where the exposed gold wefts delineate blossoming lily plants. The placement of the lilies rising from the hem and the drape of the cocoon opera coat exposing the nape of the wearer's neck were inspired by the Japanese kimono.

House of Worth
Paris, founded 1857

COAT, 1910–11
Silk cut and voided velvet on silk- and metallic-thread satin foundation with metallic lace, and jet- and glass-bead trim
Gift of Mrs. Kerckhoff Young
M.69.10
Label: C Worth

Mariano José María Bernardo Fortuny
Spain, 1871–1949, active Italy

DRESS, "DELPHOS"
Italy, c. 1915
Silk plain weave, pleated
Gift of Mrs. Evelyn Burgur
M.74.2.4

Painted and Printed Textiles

DEVELOPMENT OF THE TEXTILE-PRINTING INDUSTRY IN EUROPE in the eighteenth and nineteenth centuries is inextricably connected to the introduction of painted cotton textiles from India in the seventeenth century. The colors and motifs of Indian *pintados* (Portuguese for "painted or spotted cloth") were intriguing to Europeans for their exotic appeal. A voracious demand for these textiles had a profound impact on the economy: increasing development of international and intra-European trade, migration of skilled workers, which effectively transported technical innovation and aesthetic ideas, and, ultimately, the mechanization of textile production.

Portuguese traders encountered these distinctive cloths in India while en route to the islands of Southeast Asia to trade for their primary objective: pepper and other spices. Establishment of international trading organizations—the British East India Company in 1600, the Dutch Vereenigde Oostindische Compagnie (the Dutch East India Company) in 1602, and the French Compagnie française des Indes orientales (the French East India Company) in 1664—facilitated commerce in textiles. The market for cotton cloth accounted for a significant portion of the companies' sales; for some in the eighteenth century, it was more than half.

Europeans were drawn to the *chints* (Hindi for "sprinkling water"), *indiennes* (French for "of India"), and calicos (named for Calicut, India) for their colors, which were bright and saturated and, more importantly, permanent and washable. Textile painters and dyers of India produced brilliant, colorfast hues with the use of mordants (colorless chemical thickeners of aluminum or ferrous salts), which, when painted ("penciled") or woodblock-printed on a textile, fixed the dye permanently to the fiber. Another permanent color was indigo, a blue more vivid and versatile than European woad. In application, the pattern's other colors were covered with a liquid solution of wax (to resist the blue dye) before the cloth was placed in a vat; indigo revealed its subtle shades through a complex process of oxidation and repeat immersion.

Although fascinated by the colors and exotic "oriental" designs of the calicos, Europeans were sending specifications and

actual patterns to India to be copied as early as 1662. Even earlier, in 1648, domestic printing of calicos was established in the French city of Marseilles, which had been a leading importer, and, in 1676, in print shops in Amsterdam and London. Europe then had its own competitive industry to meet the insatiable demand for foreign cloth.

Expanded calico production posed a very serious threat to Europe's inveterate silk and wool industries. Governmental prohibitions in France in 1686 and Britain in 1701 against the importation or production of calicos were not completely effective. Bans were difficult to enforce because local regulations variously forbade or allowed reexport, made exceptions for some painted textiles, permitted prints on certain fabrics other than cotton, or allowed production in exempted cities. Because goods were smuggled and technological information migrated with skilled textile workers, and because of the general disregard of the laws by wealthy consumers, bans were lifted in France in 1759 and in Britain in 1774—with a resultant expansion of the textile-printing industry.

Although printing with wood blocks continued, engraved copperplate printing of textiles, invented by Dubliner Francis Nixon in 1755, introduced more delicate line, shading, and sculptural effects to designs. Larger plates permitted larger repeats, increasing efficiency. Entrepreneurs instituted major textile-printing factories. Four of the most successful were Christophe-Philippe Oberkampf (1738–1815) at Jouy-en-Josas, outside of Paris; Sir Robert Peel (1750–1830) at Bury, England; Samuel Koechlin (1719–1776) and Jean-Jacques Schmalzer (1721–1797) at Mulhouse, in France's Alsace region; and Johann Heinrich von Schüle (1720–1811) at Augsburg, Germany.

Roller-printing with a copper cylinder, invented in 1783 by Thomas Bell in Scotland, engendered a revolution in production—at Jouy-en-Josas, one day's yield in roller-printed yardage would have taken forty-two wood-block printers to achieve the same rate. By the end of the eighteenth century, with the help of roller-printing, the cotton gin, spinning mules, and steam engines, textile printing had emerged into the modern industrial era.

In the late seventeenth century, European men wore an at-home garment called a banyan. Made of silk (p. 58) or cotton, it was used for informal wear. Calico banyans frequently exhibit European influence on Indian cotton-painters; this banyan's convoluted columns entwined with branches, curling leaves, and urns are fundamental design elements of English crewel embroidery from the late seventeenth century.

MAN'S AT-HOME ROBE (BANYAN)
India, probably Coromandel Coast, for the Western market, 1700–1750
Cotton plain weave, mordant-painted and resist-dyed
Costume Council Fund

M.2005.42

Floral sprays set in lozenges of meandering vines with small flowers was a popular calico pattern in the 1770s and 1780s. Typical of the rococo aesthetic, it was quite different from the patterns of opulent, full-blown, decorated blossoms and foliage characteristic of those created in the first part of the eighteenth century. Although the dress was block-printed, the green areas were hand-painted with indigo brushed over yellow; a method to achieve permanent green was not invented until 1808.

DRESS (ROBE À LA FRANÇAISE)
France, c. 1770
Cotton plain weave, block-printed and dye-painted, with silk passementerie
M.2007.211.718

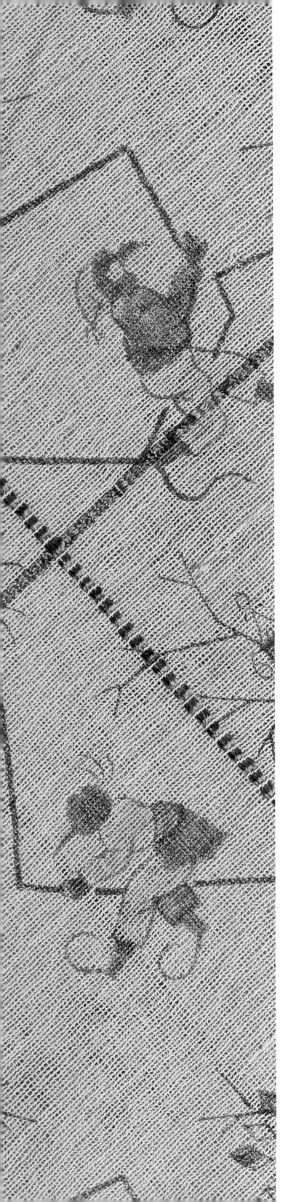

Advances in dye chemistry in the early nineteenth century included the discovery of chrome yellow, green, and orange, derived from the chromate of lead. This vivid yellow, introduced in Alsace in 1819, was an extremely popular color in Europe during the 1820s. Also a common aspect of chinoiserie for its association with royalty, yellow was a recurrent background for fanciful (and stereotypical) dancing figures with pigtails, pipes, and parasols.

DRESS
Europe, c. 1827
Silk and cotton gauze with silk supplementary warp and weft patterning, block-printed
M.2007.211.937

A cape with a wide hood, bordered with a band of extremely fine pleats, was worn by women of Provence from about 1770 to 1830. Somber *ramoneur* (chimney sweep) prints were based on Indian calicos of abstracted floral motifs or tiny naturalistic flowers scattered on a dark ground. Capes were lined in wool or with one to three different cottons printed with miniature floral or geometric patterns called mignonettes after the flower of that name.

HOODED CAPE
Provence, France, 1785–1820
Cotton plain weave, copperplate- and roller-printed
M.2007.211.669

PETTICOAT
Provence, France, 1795–1820
Silk plain weave, quilted
Gift of Mr. and Mrs. H. W. Grieve
M.79.237.7

PAIR OF SHOES
England, 1790–95
Silk satin and leather
Gift of Mrs. Hazel Steadman Brukhardt
16.20.3A–B

Tailoring

Tailoring transforms flat textiles into three-dimensional garments. The term is derived from the French *tailler*, meaning simply "to cut." However, the garments (and undergarments) in this section have been manipulated through a vast array of sophisticated construction techniques. Many of these techniques were employed to create or reduce bulk according to the demands of fashion and vanity; others showed off expensive textiles and trimmings.

In the eighteenth century, a garment's tailoring was much less important—and less expensive—than its materials. External opulence often masked haphazard construction. An outwardly beautiful garment might be lined with a patchwork of scraps, or a different garment altogether. Plain but functional items such as linen shirts, which had to endure frequent washing, were more carefully stitched than silk gowns, which eventually would be unpicked to be altered or "turned" (resewn with the reverse side of the textile facing outward, to prolong the life of the unwashable garment). Because fabric was so valuable, it was customarily recycled, and clothes were not constructed to last as long as their textiles.

Traditionally, male tailors made complex garments with high price tags: men's suits, women's boned corsets and hoop petticoats, riding habits, and court gowns. Seamstresses, by contrast, produced women's dresses and children's clothing. But these professional and gendered boundaries were highly contested, and in the late eighteenth century professional seamstresses won the right to make boned undergarments and some menswear. For most women, sewing was not a profession or a hobby but an everyday household chore. Girls learned to sew at a very young age; even wealthy women practiced embroidery and other forms of needlework.

In the late eighteenth century, the French Revolution and the influence of English sportswear shifted fashion's emphasis from color, embellishment, and texture to tailoring, particularly for menswear. Clothes were expected not only to fit but also flatter the body, emphasizing the fashionable silhouette and concealing physical imperfections. Innovative tools and techniques permitted a closer fit, while new ways of cinching, padding, and pleating altered volume and proportion. When textiles had been the focus of fashion in the previous century, they were cut and sewn as little as possible; now tailors and dressmakers used seaming and shaping to mold textiles to the body.

By the mid-1800s, sewing machines, paper patterns, and inexpensive fashion magazines had revolutionized home dressmaking. Professional seamstresses also made use of the new technology, though high-end garments continued to be hand-stitched, as early sewing machines could make only straight seams.

With few exceptions, all the objects in this publication are one of a kind, custom-made for specific people who lived privileged lifestyles and had unique bodies; relatively little clothing was mass-produced before the late nineteenth century. Although ready-to-wear existed in the eighteenth century, it was slow to develop because of the difficulties associated with fit; standardized sizes did not become commonplace until the twentieth century.

Some garments have telltale signs of being handmade; others have such fine, regular stitches that it is hard to believe they are not machine sewn. Their makers are, for the most part, anonymous, but they have left tantalizing evidence of their effort and artistry.

Women's gowns of the eighteenth century were constructed
in three separate pieces: the over-
gown, a triangular insert called
a stomacher, and the petticoat.
The stomacher was pinned or
stitched into place at the time of
dressing rather than permanently
attached, so it could be worn
with different gowns. The deep
"winged" cuffs and bell-shaped
skirt of this *robe à la française*
date it to the 1740s.

**DRESS AND PETTICOAT (ROBE À LA
FRANÇAISE)**
Europe, c. 1745
Silk plain weave (shot taffeta)
M.2007.211.927A–B

STOMACHER
England, c. 1735
Silk satin with silk and metallic-
thread embroidery, metallic-thread
passementerie, and twisted-cord trim
M.2007.211.126

Fashionable eighteenth-century corsets were shaped with a series of meticulously stitched, extremely narrow channels inserted with strips of flexible, lightweight baleen or whalebone (the hardened hairlike fibers lining the roof of a baleen whale's mouth). They were tightly laced at the back and stiffened in the front with a busk—a strip of bone, metal, or wood. Decorated at the front, corsets such as this one were meant to be visible.

CORSET
France, c. 1730–40
Silk plain weave with supplementary weft-float patterning
Gift of Mr. Jack Cole
63.24.5

The hoop petticoat or *panier* (French for basket), worn in Europe in the early eighteenth century, measured up to six feet in width by midcentury. Strips of cane or baleen formed an expanded oval with extra hoops on the sides to maintain the garment's amplitude. The exaggerated breadth of the *panier* was meant to enhance the artificially long and slender corseted bodice, and to support and display wide skirts made of expensive textiles.

HOOP PETTICOAT
England, 1750–80
Linen plain weave and cane
M.2007.211.981

CORSET
England, c. 1780
Linen twill and baleen
M.2007.211.353

CHEMISE
England, 1775–1800
Cotton plain weave
M.2007.211.428

PAIR OF SHOES
Germany or Italy, 1770–80
Silk plain weave with silk supplementary weft-float patterning, silk plain-weave trim, and leather
Mrs. Alice F. Schott Bequest
M.67.8.125A–B

By the 1780s, the *robe à l'anglaise* (English-style gown), with its closely fitted back, had replaced the flowing *robe à la française* (French-style gown) for all but the most formal occasions. This example has two narrow center-back panels that extend from the neckline to the hem without a waist seam, a tailoring technique known as *en fourreau* (as a sheath). The slim fit of the bodice is offset by a billowing skirt, which has been cartridge-pleated for maximum fullness, creating an elegant deep V at the back.

DRESS (ROBE À L'ANGLAISE)
France, 1785–90
Silk twill and silk plain-weave stripes
M.2007.211.931

FICHU
England, 1750–1800
Cotton plain weave (muslin) with cotton embroidery
Costume Council Fund
M.80.190.5

Because the long, full skirts of eighteenth-century dresses were not always practical, women frequently tucked the corners of their overgowns into their side-pocket openings for ease of movement. In the 1770s, internal systems of cloth tapes and loops were added to raise the overskirt, dividing it into three distinct draped sections. The style was called the *robe à la polonaise* (Polish-style gown) to commemorate the 1772 partition of Poland into three territories under Austrian, Prussian, and Russian rule.

DRESS (ROBE À LA POLONAISE)
France, c. 1775
Silk plain weave with supplementary warp- and weft-float patterning
Gift of Mrs. Derek A. Colls in memory of Mrs. Joanna Christie Crawford
M.70.85

PETTICOAT
England, 1780s
Silk plain weave, quilted
Costume Council Fund
M.59.25C

HAT (BERGÈRE)
France, c. 1760
Straw, cotton plain weave, and silk plain-weave ribbon with supplementary weft-float patterning trim
Purchased with funds provided by Mrs. H. Grant Theis and Nelly Llanos Kilroy
M.2001.56

FICHU
Europe, 1750–1800
Cotton plain weave (muslin) with linen embroidery
M.2007.211.479

PAIR OF SHOES
England, 1780–85
Silk plain weave with silk supplementary weft-float patterning, silk plain weave with silk warp- and weft-float patterning, silk satin, and leather
Costume Council Fund
M.81.71.3A–B

Label: Edmond Turner / Shoe Maker / Roxbury Street

This early tailcoat, with its high collar, wide lapels, short front, and long back, was influenced by English riding coats and would later be adopted and exaggerated by French fashion extremists (*incroyables*). The sleeves, set unnaturally close together, forced the wearer to hold his shoulders back and thrust his chest forward. Layering vests and wearing a large cravat further enhanced this silhouette.

COAT
France, c. 1790–95
Silk and cotton plain weave and silk satin stripes
M.2007.211.802

VEST
France, c. 1790–95
Silk plain weave with supplementary weft-float patterning, and silk and metallic-thread passementerie
M.2007.211.1080

VEST
France, 1790–95
Silk plain weave with supplementary weft patterning
M.2007.211.1081

BREECHES
France, 1790–95
Cotton plain weave
M.2007.211.1082

The redingote—a French corruption of "riding coat"— was a dress resembling an Englishman's greatcoat. It typically had wide lapels, large buttons, and long, tight sleeves. This example also incorporates a cape collar (p. 14) and six buttons at the center back. It is cut away at the front in imitation of the tailcoats worn by men at the time. A false front conceals a tightly laced inner closure and mirrors the inflated upper-body silhouette of men's fashion.

DRESS (REDINGOTE)
Europe, c. 1790
Silk and cotton satin and plain weave
Purchased with funds provided by Robert and Mary M. Looker
M.2009.120

FICHU
England, 1780–95
Cotton plain weave (muslin) with cotton embroidery
M.2007.211.494

The spencer, with its high neckline and long sleeves, provided much-needed warmth when worn with lightweight neoclassical gowns. It was named for George, 2nd Earl Spencer (1758–1834), who removed the tails from one of his coats in the mid-1790s. After a brief, unflattering life as a male garment, the spencer became a fashionable female garment in the early nineteenth century. The Renaissance-style puffed oversleeves on this example reflect the contemporary taste for historicism.

JACKET (SPENCER) AND PETTICOAT
France, c. 1815
Jacket: cotton plain weave; skirt: cotton plain weave with linen net and cotton plain-weave appliqués
M.2007.211.15A–B

PAIR OF BOOTS
England, c. 1810
Leather with metal buckles
M.2007.211.298A–B

Rudolph Ackermann
Walking Dress, No. 23. of R. Ackermann's Repository of Arts (detail), November 1, 1817
Fashion plate: hand-colored engraving on paper
Gift of Charles LeMaire, Doris Stein Research Center, LACMA

The voluminous beret sleeves of this evening dress were cut from large circular pieces of fabric, lined with stiff woven horsehair, and folded into a series of calculated knife pleats. The oppositional direction of the pleats creates an architectural effect. Interior cloth ties adjust the fullness of the sleeves to the wearer's preference.

DRESS
England, c. 1830
Silk plain weave (organza) and silk satin with imitation-pearl glass beads
M.2007.211.940A–B

PAIR OF SHOES
Vienna, Austria, c. 1840
Silk satin with silk embroidery and leather
Mrs. Alice F. Schott Bequest
M.67.8.154A–B

Joseph Robins
Paris, Ball Dress. Joseph Robins, Bride Court. London (detail)
From *Ladies Pocket Magazine*, c. 1830
Fashion plate: hand-colored engraving on paper
Gift of Dr. and Mrs. Gerald Labiner, Doris Stein Research Center, LACMA

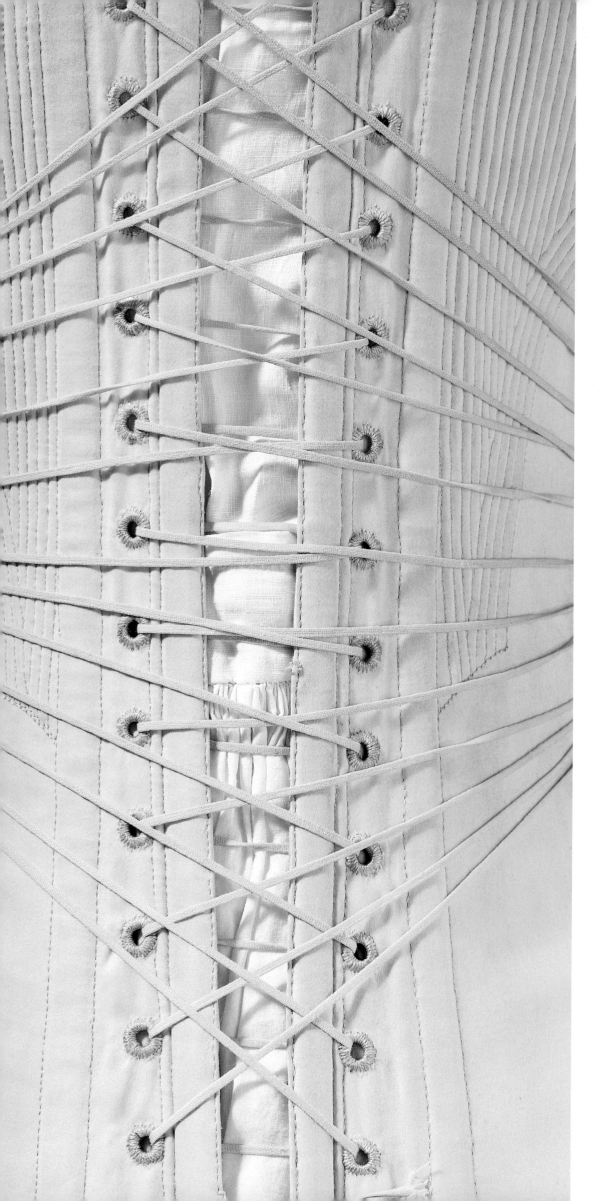

The hourglass silhouette of the 1830s was implemented by a longer corset boned with baleen and further stiffened with a wide steel busk. A new system of crossed ties allowed the wearer to lace her own corset without assistance. Ballooning dress sleeves required the lightweight, resilient support of sleeve plumpers, "pillows" filled with down or feathers. Wide skirts were supported by multiple petticoats shaped with pin-tucks, cording, or novelty weaves.

(OPPOSITE, LEFT)

PAIR OF SLEEVE PLUMPERS
England, 1830–35
Linen plain weave with down fill
M.2007.211.440A–B

CHEMISE
Europe, 1835
Linen plain weave
M.2007.211.447

CORSET
England, 1830–40
Cotton sateen, quilted, with cotton twill and cotton plain-weave tape
Costume Council Fund
M.63.54.7

PETTICOAT
Europe, 1830–35
Cotton plain weave with supplementary weft-float patterning
M.2007.211.442

PAIR OF SHOES
France, c. 1835
Silk satin and leather
M.2007.211.314A–B

*Illustration after Devéria
(Le Coucher), 1829*

The fullness of the sleeves on this dress (below, right) was distributed through the length of the arm, in a style called balloon, *à l'imbécile* (silly), or *à la folle* (foolish). The hem was finished by folding and tacking the wide scalloped edge to the outside, revealing the embroidery.

DRESS
Europe, c. 1830
Cotton plain weave (muslin) with cutwork and cotton embroidery
M.2007.211.739

BONNET
Europe, c. 1830
Straw with silk-ribbon trim
M.2007.211.167

BAG (RETICULE)
France, 1800–1825
Silk plain weave with sequins and silk embroidery
M.2007.211.253

PAIR OF SHOES
France, 1830–40
Silk satin and leather
M.2007.211.304A–B

Label: A Paris / No. 22 Rue de la Paix / second Magasin a gauche / par le Boulevard / MELNOTTE / B. de L.L. MM la Reine des / Francais et la Reine des Belges / 164 Regent street / London

The art of tailoring made significant advances in the second quarter of the nineteenth century, with the highly engineered tailcoat becoming an essential element of menswear. The secret of the tailcoat's smooth, elegant exterior was its intricately pad-stitched interior. Wool was the tailor's fabric of choice, as it could be stretched, shrunk, or shaped using friction and heat to create a precise fit, as seen in the way the sleeve cap is shaped to fit neatly into the armscye. M-notches ensured a flawless transition from the close-fitting drape of the collar to the wide lapels.

COAT
Scotland, c. 1845
Wool plain weave, full finish
M.2007.211.958

TROUSERS
Scotland, c. 1845
Cotton twill
M.2007.211.959

TOP HAT
France, 1825–50
Beaver fur
M.2007.211.705

The quest for a narrow waistline was not exclusive to women; in the early nineteenth century, some men also wore boned and tightly laced corsets. Because vests were short, modified waist cinchers or firmly stiffened belts continued to be worn throughout the century to minimize unsightly bulges that blemished the streamlined effect of fine tailoring.

MAN'S WAIST BINDER
England, 1894
Silk satin, quilted, cotton-twill trim
and belt with metal buckle
M.2007.211.648

Label: "strozona" / fielders patent /
british & colonial industrial exhibition. /
manchester 1894. / republique / française. /
awarded / four / gold / medals / and / cross
of / honour / paris 1894

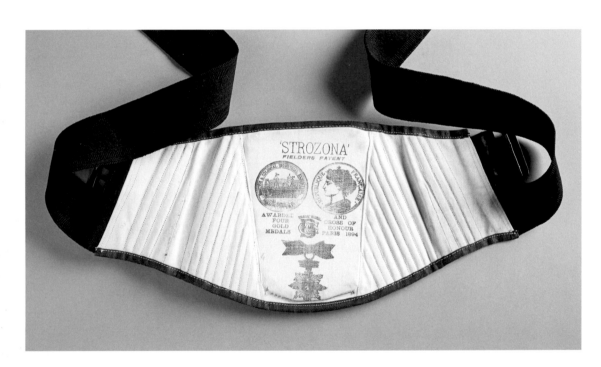

By design, the stripes in this vest point diagonally from the shoulder to the center front, fostering the illusion of a broad chest narrowing into a tapered waist. In reality, extra padding created the fashionable "barrel" chest. To achieve the silhouette, this vest was constructed with open front spaces between the outside and the lining into which variable thicknesses of padding could be inserted.

VEST WITH REMOVABLE CHEST PADS
England, c. 1840
Vest: silk satin with supplementary weft-float patterning; pads: cotton twill with cotton wadding

M.2007.211.823

The simple but dramatic lines of this two-piece dress are designed to show off the lacelike patterned silk. The sweep of the bell-shaped skirt is echoed in the pagoda sleeves (named for the Asian tiered tower), which open to reveal separate undersleeves. The triangular shape of the heavily boned bodice tapering into a deep point at the waist is reflected in the crinoline-supported skirt, making the twenty-two-inch waistline appear even smaller.

DRESS
France, c. 1855
Silk plain weave with supplementary weft-float patterning, silk satin, and silk-ribbon trim
M.2007.211.29A–B

COLLAR
Europe, 1845–50
Cotton plain weave (muslin) with cotton embroidery
M.2007.211.572

PAIR OF UNDERSLEEVES
Europe or United States, c. 1855
Cotton plain weave with cotton cutwork embroidery (*broderie anglaise*)
M.2007.211.622A–B

The Bessemer Process, patented
in 1855, greatly increased the
malleability of steel, making
possible a flexible steel-wire
armature (cage crinoline) to
replace the bulk of numerous
petticoats. This lightweight
steel skeleton allowed skirts to
widen to excessive proportions,
recalling the extremities of the
mid-eighteenth-century *panier*.
Dome-shaped in 1856, the cage
became pyramid-shaped in the
early 1860s, when style dictated
that the massive skirts be swept
to the garment's back.

CAGE CRINOLINE
England, c. 1865
Cotton-braid-covered steel, cotton
twill and plain-weave double-cloth
tape, cane, and metal
M.2007.211.380

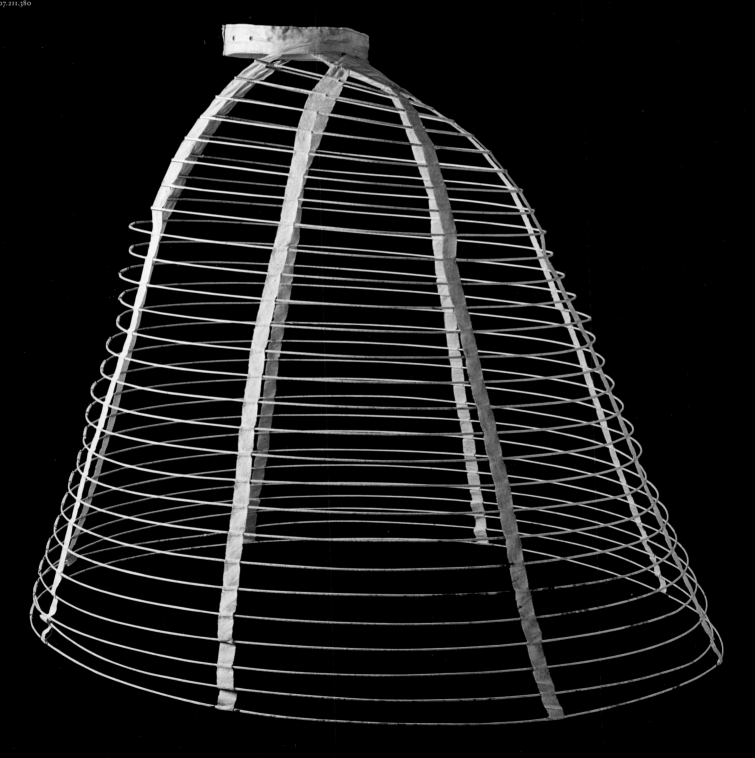

Seaside Fashion

Eugène-Louis Boudin
Approaching Storm, 1864
Oil on cradled panel
Mr. and Mrs. Lewis Larnd Coburn
Memorial Collection, The Art
Institute of Chicago

WEALTHY EUROPEANS HAVE BEEN TRAVELING TO THE SEASIDE for the health benefits of the fresh air and bracing water since the eighteenth century. The expansion of the railways in the mid-nineteenth century also made it possible for the newly prosperous middle class to escape stifling, polluted cities for the coast. Quiet fishing villages were transformed into luxurious beachfront resorts, where musicians, artists, and entrepreneurs congregated every summer to entertain tourists clad in garments specially designed for the seaside.

The Normandy coast, only a few hours from Paris by train, drew fashionable Parisians who brought their urban elegance to the boardwalks of Trouville, Deauville, and Dieppe. On the other side of the English Channel, Londoners flocked to the new pleasure piers at Brighton, Bournemouth, and Margate.

Most of these tourists were content to sit and stroll along the shore, fully clothed. Bathers climbed into wheeled huts on the beach, where they changed into ankle-length wool garments worn with hats, stockings, and slippers. Horses pulled these "bathing machines" to the water's edge, allowing bathers to slip directly into the water without being seen so scantily clad.

In and out of the water, seaside garments were less formal and more daring and frivolous than the fashions worn in town. Indeed, these outfits "would produce the greatest consternation if worn anywhere else but at the sea-side."[12] They incorporated textiles and trimmings suitable for the coastal climate and lifestyle. Sun, sand, and salt typically ruined one's clothes by the end of a summer season, so seaside fashions were inexpensive and washable; they were constructed simply and not built to last. At the same time, they reflected current trends, including the crinoline and bustle silhouettes; their very disposability made them more susceptible to changing fashions.

Here, a loose jacket called a *paletot* is worn over a matching, fitted bodice and skirt. In June 1861, *The Englishwoman's Domestic Magazine* declared: "The *paletot* is the favorite shape for light cloth cloaks for sea-side and country wear."

This ensemble is made of a lightweight but stiff ribbed cotton called piqué at the time, which was popular for summer dresses. In addition to reflecting the sunlight, white clothing masked salt stains. William Taylor, a visitor to Brighton in 1837, recorded in his diary after a blustery day at the seaside: "My hat is as white as though I had rolled it in the salt tub."[13]

White and navy (named for the dark blue uniforms of Britain's Royal Navy) was a common color combination for seaside dress, which often was embellished with stripes, anchors, and other nautical details. Here, navy embroidery is copiously but economically applied by machine in geometric and stylized floral motifs.

SEASIDE ENSEMBLE
France, 1864–67
Cotton plain weave with
supplementary warp, and cotton
machine embroidery
M.2007.211.944A–C

SEASIDE HAT
Probably England, c. 1870
Straw with ostrich feathers, crimped
cotton plain weave, glass beads, and
silk-velvet ribbon
Costume Council Fund
M.64.85.5

With the decrease in circumference and popularity of
the oversize cage crinoline,
a narrower, lighter, conical
version became fashionable in
the 1860s. Bright colors from
recently introduced aniline dyes
were favored for the "American"
cage, a hoop petticoat partially
covered with fabric. The
corset's restrictive rigidity was
maintained with steam-molding,
patented in 1868. Various waist
sizes were available in corsets
heavily starched, steamed,
and dried on metal or ceramic
idealized torsos.

CORSET
England, 1865–75
Cotton plain weave with
cotton lace trim
M.2007.211.360

CHEMISE
England, 1850–70
Linen plain weave with cotton cutwork
embroidery (*broderie anglaise*) and
cotton lace
M.2007.211.427

CAGE CRINOLINE
England, 1862–70
Wool twill, cotton plain weave with
stamped grid pattern, cotton-twill
tape, cotton-braid-covered steel,
and metal
M.2007.211.386

PAIR OF SHOES
Europe, c. 1870
Leather
M.2007.211.712A–B

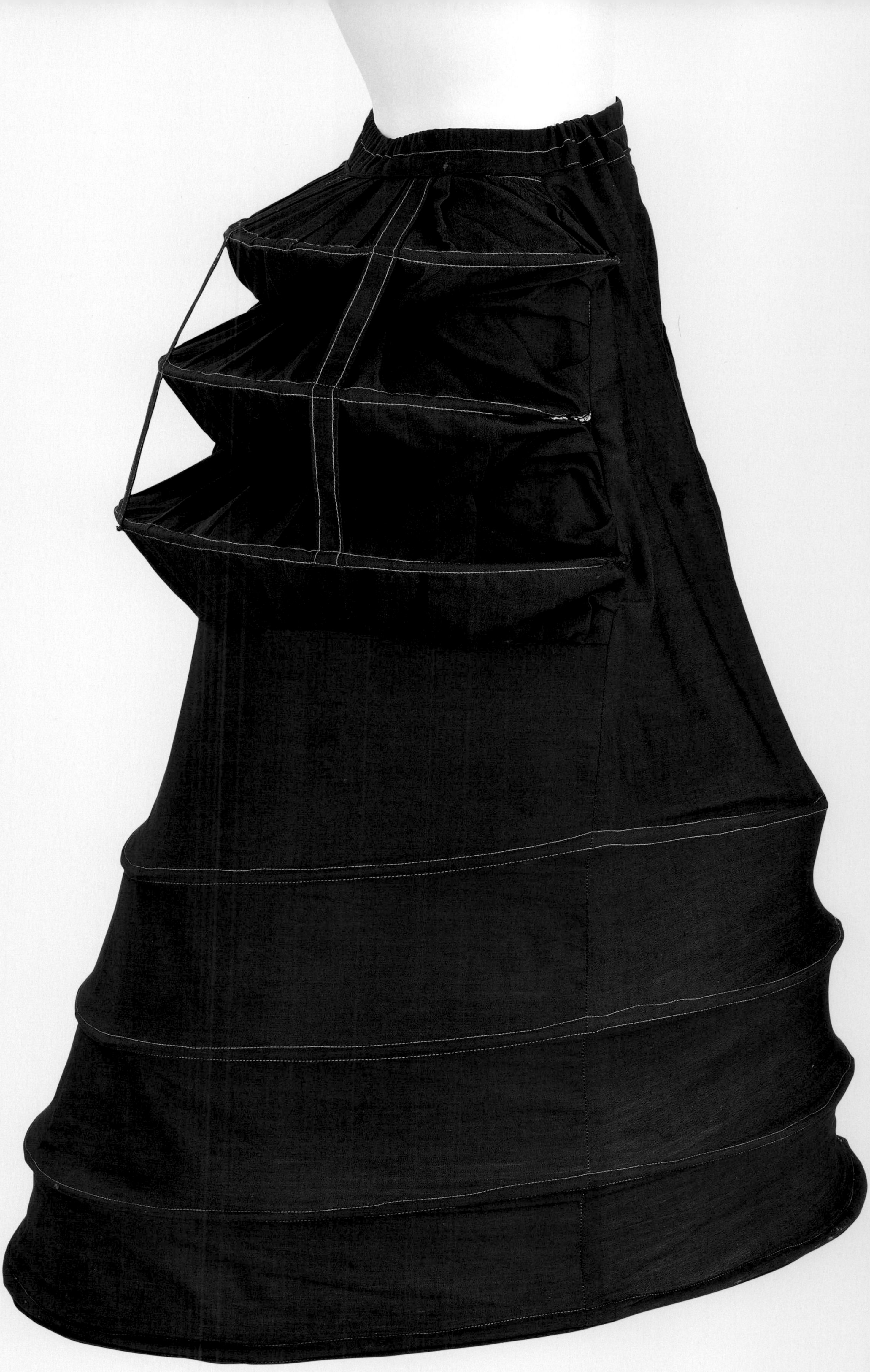

To accommodate the upward sweep of skirts to the back, a hybrid crinoline with bustle, the crinolette, was invented to support the billowing drapery of still-massive skirts. Some retained a conical shape with short posterior hoops; others were closed flat in the front with a series of half hoops at the back. Attached ties regulated the tension and adjusted the petticoat's fullness.

CRINOLETTE
England, 1872–75
Cotton and wool twill with steel
M.2007.211.387
Label: Harpers Improved / Registered
Pannier Jupon

CRINOLETTE
England, 1872–75
Wool plain weave, cotton plain weave, cotton-braid-covered steel, cotton-twill tape, and wool-braid trim
M.2007.211.388

With the widespread use of the sewing machine, dressmaking grew more complex, as illustrated in this two-piece bodice-and-skirt ensemble. The fitted bodice required many pattern pieces, including a decorative peplum (center-back extension) that rested on the bustle. The asymmetrical skirt is constructed of multiple pieces of fabric manipulated into folds and decorated with trim.

DRESS
England, c. 1885
Silk plain weave with warp-float and supplementary weft patterning, and silk satin
M.2007.211.781A–B

BONNET
Paris, c. 1885
Straw with silk velvet
Gift of Mrs. Edwin Greble
29.5.214

The fashion for commodious bustles in the late 1870s and 1880s created a demand for a variety of shapes and sizes. Auxiliary bustles were crafted with horsehair, padding, and hoops of baleen or steel. Although comfort had never been a prerequisite for structural underwear, the hinged wire bustle (center) was ingeniously conceived to collapse when the wearer was seated and to resume its original shape when she arose.

BUSTLE
England, c. 1875
Cotton and horsehair plain weave with cotton-twill tape trim
M.2007.211.392

BUSTLE
England, c. 1885
Metal and cotton-twill tape
M.2007.211.400

BUSTLE
England, c. 1875
Cotton and horsehair plain weave, and cotton-twill trim with stamped gold pattern
M.2007.211.394

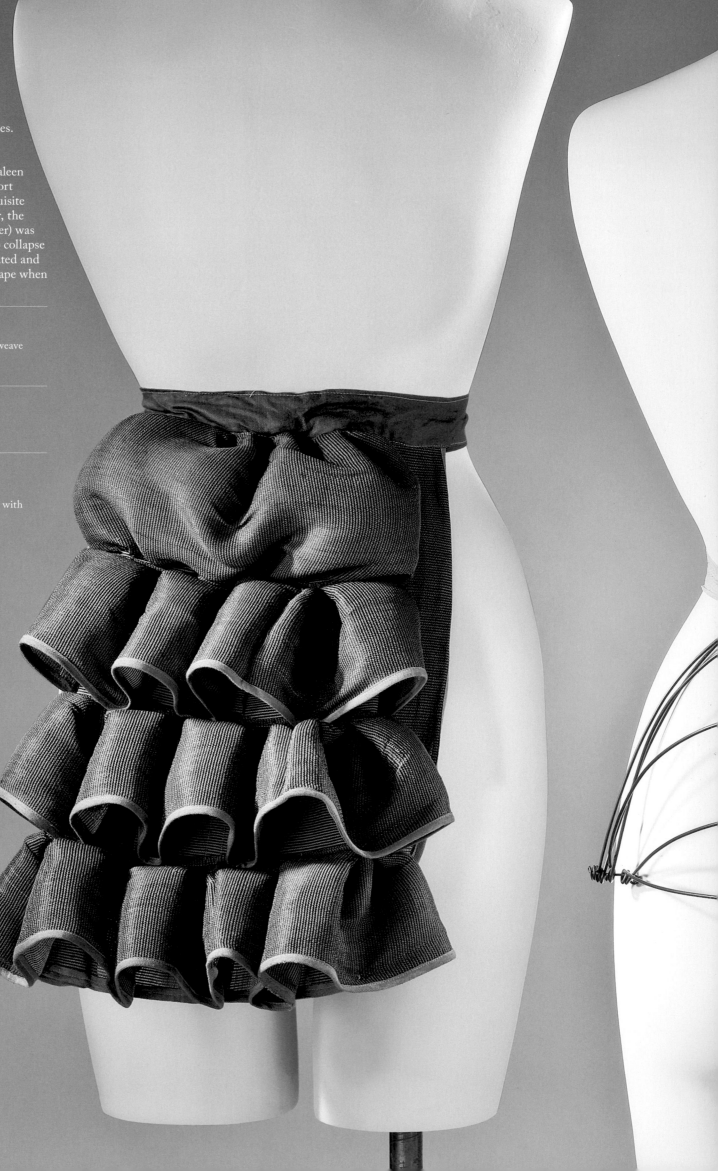

Tennis Dressing

LAWN TENNIS FIRST BECAME POPULAR IN ENGLAND in the early
1870s. Along with croquet and horseback riding, it was one of the few
sports that men and women could play together, and it was enjoyed
primarily by the leisured upper class. Therefore, female players were
expected to dress attractively and fashionably as well as practically.
Scottish novelist and essayist Margaret Oliphant (1828–1897)
complained that while men wore special clothes for tennis, women
wore "a dress perhaps, but not always, a little shorter and simpler than
ordinary."[14] It was not unusual to see women in high collars, long
sleeves, corsets, and even bustles on the tennis court.

While following the fashionable silhouette of the mid-1880s, this
tennis dress makes small concessions to the physical rigors of playing
tennis. It is made of lightweight, washable cotton, with a comparatively
short skirt and a deep pocket for holding tennis balls. Though there
was a burgeoning market for comfortable "sport" bustles, this dress
has a built-in bustle with interior ties to adjust the volume (opposite,
detail), which eliminated the need for a separate understructure. These
innovations distinguish such garments from everyday fashions.

In dress as well as behavior, lawn tennis changed the rules for
women off the court. In 1885 the magazine *The Field* reported: "Lawn
tennis has taught women how much they are capable of doing, and it
is a sign of the times that various games and sports which would have
been tabooed a few years ago as 'unladylike' are actually encouraged at
various girls' schools."

Sir John Lavery, RA, RSA
The Tennis Party, 1885
Oil on canvas
Presented in 1926 by Sir James Murray,
Aberdeen Art Gallery & Museums

TENNIS DRESS
England, c. 1885
Cotton plain weave, printed, with
cotton-lace trim
M.2007.211.782A–B

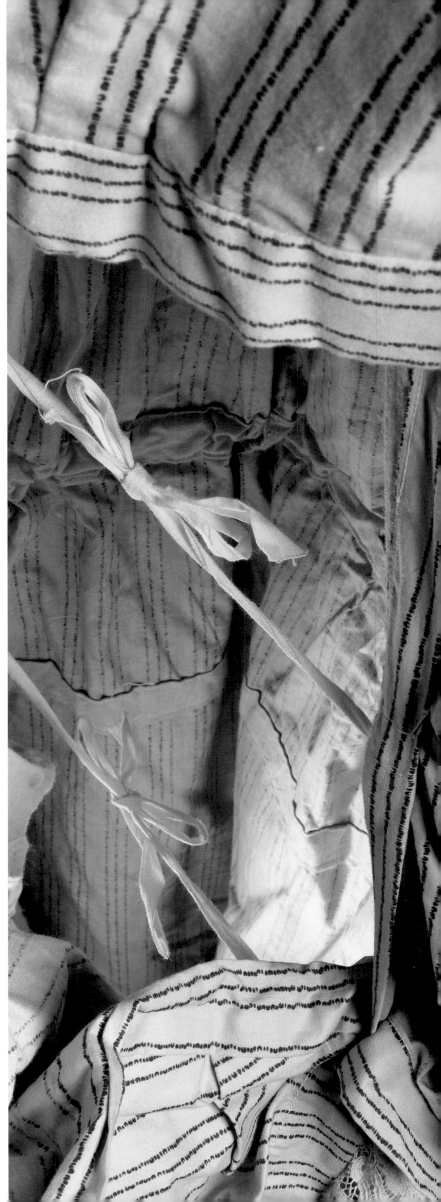

For centuries, wool fabric in various woven techniques and thicknesses has been utilized in a wide range of garments—from military uniforms to fashionable dress for both men and women. This dolman, an outer garment with sleeves that are set into armscyes that extend to the waist, is tailored to be worn over a bustled dress. The wool twill is similar in woven structure and pattern to that used for men's suits.

COAT (DOLMAN)
England, c. 1885
Wool twill
M.2007.211.780

BONNET
Europe, c. 1880
Straw with silk velvet, ostrich feathers, metallic buckle, and silk satin ribbon trim
M.2007.211.659

The columnar "princess line," probably named for the glamorous and famously slim Princess Alexandra of Wales, was introduced in 1875. The construction of a fitted, one-piece dress without a waistline seam—shaped by long darts from bust to hips—was a milestone in tailoring. The term *princess line* outlasted this confining style and is still used today.

Mademoiselles Giroux
France, active c. 1880

DRESS
Limoges, France, c. 1880
Silk plain weave (taffeta) with silk ribbon and silk-knotted trim

M.2007.211.35

Label: MELLES GIROUX 7 RUE DU PORTAIL IMBERT LIMOGES

Tallyho!

Sir John Everett Millais, *Trust Me*, 1862, The Forbes Galleries

FAMOUSLY DESCRIBED BY OSCAR WILDE in *A Woman of No Importance* as "the unspeakable in full pursuit of the uneatable," foxhunting evolved from a form of rural pest control into an upper-class social ritual in the late eighteenth century. The traditional clothing worn by participants reflects the sport's origins as the pastime of the English country gentleman, and it has remained relatively unchanged for two hundred years.

This iconic coat likely was worn by John Hamilton of Sundrum, a town in southwest Scotland, in the late 1820s. It combines practicality with the luxury of skilled tailoring (p. 2) and expensive materials, and it captures the historical moment when hunting attire began to diverge from fashionable dress. Previously, hunters had worn ordinary, fashionable clothing adapted for convenience and efficiency. When the sport of foxhunting was regulated and codified in the early nineteenth century, hunting clothes became frozen in time and have changed slowly, if at all, since then.

A foxhunter's chief adversary was not the fox but the elements. An overcoat would have been cumbersome on horseback; instead, hunters wore close-fitting garments made of warm, weatherproof materials. Beaver-fur hats, thick wool coats, buckskin breeches, and high leather boots protected hunters from the soggy British climate.

"Hunting pinks," as they were called from the late 1820s, were actually scarlet coats; they are thought to have been named for Thomas Pink, a London tailor. Red made hunters visible to one another, and may have alluded to the sport's royal or military antecedents. The cutaway coat, or tailcoat, crossed over from riding dress into fashion in the 1790s; by the 1840s, it had gone out of style as an everyday garment, though it continues to be worn for hunting and formal wear today.

The shirt collar is held closed by a stock, a neck cloth that buckles in back. First worn by military men in the eighteenth century, the stock supported the neck and was less likely to hinder movement than a long cravat.

Though breeches had gone out of fashion for everyday dress by 1810, they remained in use at court (where their survival was a measure of their formality) and for riding because they were more comfortable than trousers on horseback. This pair is made of white buckskin for durability and protection from the elements. A hunting manual of 1839 recommended leather breeches "because they are almost everlasting, and, therefore, though double the price at first, are cheapest and best in the end."[15]

Because breeches left the calves unprotected, boots were essential. Since the 1760s, horsemen have worn knee-high black-leather boots folded down to show contrasting tan linings, called top boots. It was difficult to keep top boots clean, and contemporary etiquette books often included advice on polishing them. One popular recipe involved polishing the bottoms with a mixture of port wine and black currant jelly, and the tops with a similar mixture of champagne and apricot jam.

The gilt buttons bear the name of the wearer's hunt, the Ayrshire Hunt, and a picture of a fox. The buttons are typical of those worn by hunt members from the eighteenth century to the present. The title character of R. S. Surtees's 1853 novel, *Mr. Sponge's Sporting Tour*, wears "a plain scarlet [coat] with a crimson velvet collar, and a bright fox on the frosted ground of a gilt button." The author poked fun at these "matter-of-fact storytelling buttons—a fox with 'TALLY-HO,' or a fox's head grinning in grim death—making a red coat look like a miniature butcher's [slaughterhouse]."[16]

Foxhunters continue to wear scarlet coats with gilt buttons, stocks, breeches, and top boots to this day; however, their quarry is often an artificially laid fox scent rather than an actual fox. In 2005 Britain's Parliament banned the controversial practice.

Man's Ensemble

HUNTING JACKET
Scotland, 1825–30
Wool plain weave, full finish
M.2007.211.956

VEST
England, 1830–40
Cotton plain weave (piqué)
M.2007.211.1067

RIDING BREECHES
Europe, 1825–30
Buckskin
M.2007.211.1040

TOP HAT
United States, 1840–60
S. Tuttle Hat & Cap Manufacturer
Beaver fur
M.2007.211.828

STOCK
Europe, c. 1840
Silk plain weave (faille)
M.2007.211.971

PAIR OF BOOTS
Europe, c. 1850
Leather
M.2007.211.318A–B

Equestrian ensembles for women consisted of a hat, fitted bodice, sidesaddle skirt, and boots. Inspired by menswear, female riding habits were constructed using techniques similar to those employed to make men's suits. Women typically commissioned tailors, rather than dressmakers, to create their riding habits. Loops of twill tape sewn inside the asymmetrical skirt hooked under the wearer's instep ensured that her legs remained covered while riding.

Woman's Ensemble

RIDING HABIT
Europe, c. 1890
Wool twill, full finish
M.2007.211.879A–C

HAT (BOWLER)
England, c. 1890
Lock & Co.
London, founded 1676
Wool felt
M.2007.211.848

The tea gown—a loose, informal gown worn at home for afternoon entertaining—was a European innovation, inspired by traditional Asian garments. While some tea gowns appropriated the flowing lines of the Japanese kimono, this example's intricate tailoring and interior boning are strictly Western in origin. It is the kimonolike crossover bodice and luxurious silks that evoke the East. Contrasting plain and patterned textiles create the illusion of a two-piece ensemble. Historicizing details (such as the cape sleeves) and muted colors popularized by the aesthetic movement were hallmarks of the Liberty & Co. department store, still in existence today.

Liberty & Co.
London, 1875–present

DRESS (TEA GOWN), C. 1887

Silk twill with supplementary weft-float patterning

M.2007.211.901

Label: Liberty & Co. / ARTISTIC & HISTORIC COSTUME STUDIO / 22 Regent St. W.

The elongated hourglass silhouette of the 1890s was achieved by the revival of the leg-of-mutton sleeve and the introduction of the gored skirt, in which triangular pieces of cloth created a smooth, graceful A-line. In this example, a wide band of black velvet emphasizes the narrow waist (p. 10). The House of Rouff was known for impeccably crafted clothing, demonstrated here by the sculptural collar and cuffs, layered and pleated bodice, and interior boning.

House of Rouff
Paris, founded 1884

DRESS, c. 1897
Silk twill and silk cut velvet on twill foundation
M.2007.211.37A–B

Label: Rouff / 13 Bd HAUSSMANN PARIS

BONNET
Europe, c. 1895
Straw with silk-grosgrain ribbon
M.2007.211.661

PARASOL
Europe, c. 1890
Silk satin, wood, and metal
Anonymous gift
TR.7758.406

In the 1890s, the corset's top edge lowered, and the front busk lengthened and straightened to compress the abdomen and redirect its fullness toward the chest, simultaneously pushing the derriere back into the pronounced S-curve perceived at the time as graceful and alluring. Luxurious underwear was also de rigueur—silks, lace, a heart-shaped sachet, and beribboned garters contrasted with this corset's rigid boning.

CORSET
Probably Europe, c. 1895
Silk plain weave with supplementary warp-float patterning, linen lace, silk plain-weave ribbon, silk satin ribbon, silk braid, and metal
Mrs. Alice F. Schott Bequest
CR.448.67–131

Drawstrings on the interior pockets allowed the "bust improver," or "bosom friend," to be stuffed proportionately to achieve the full-breasted look of the stylish S-curve's monobosom. The fashionable evolution of the bustline included a number of ingenious augmentation devices, constructed from materials such as cotton batting, wax, papier-mâché, inflatable rubber, celluloid, and molded wire.

BUST IMPROVER
England, c. 1900
Cotton plain weave with cotton lace and silk satin ribbon trim
M.2007.211.369

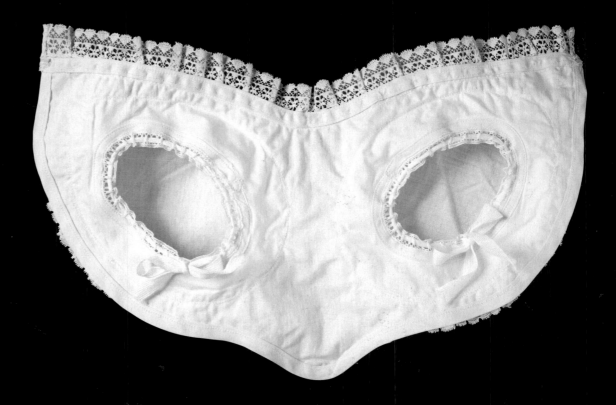

The feminine S-curve of this two-piece dress was achieved with built-in boning hidden beneath the diaphanous drape of the fashionable monobosom. The cutouts in the brown wool at the bodice and sleeves expose a series of curvilinear shapes of lace over pink crepe in the prevailing aesthetic of art nouveau. The skirt is constructed with a series of gores that flare to the floor, detailed with rows of pin-tucks and velvet appliqués that would have called attention to the undulating movement of the dress as the wearer swept by.

DRESS
France, c. 1900
Wool twill, full finish, with linen lace, silk crepe, silk velvet, and cotton plain-weave trim
M.2007.211.787A–B

CORSET
England, c. 1900
Leather and metal
M.2007.211.367

CHEMISE
United States, c. 1900
Cotton plain weave with cotton-lace
and silk-ribbon trim
Gift of Mrs. William Tidmarch
CR.418.67.2

OPEN DRAWERS
France or United States, 1891
Silk plain weave with silk-lace trim
and silk-grosgrain-ribbon ties
Gift of Mrs. George W. Briggs
62.34.3B

PAIR OF FETISH BOOTS
Belgium, c. 1900
Leather
M.2007.211.337A–B
Label: MADE IN BELGIUM ESPECIALLY
FOR / Regent Shoe Stores / 31. WARDOUR ST.
SHAFTESBURY AVENUE / LONDON W. 1.

Henri de Toulouse-Lautrec
Conquête de passage, 1896
Oil, chalk, and charcoal on paper
Musée des Augustins, Musée des
Beaux-Arts de la ville de Toulouse

Intimate scenes of the Parisian demimonde (world of courtesans) so evocatively painted in the late nineteenth century by artists such as Henri de Toulouse-Lautrec (1864–1901) confirm the erotic symbolism of the corset's dual nature of restraint and release. A corset (p. 23) or boot with a disproportionately large number of laces to tie implies an equal number to untie—extending the erotically charged process of undressing. For some, restrictive corsets and high heels provoked sexual associations with bondage and domination.

PAIR OF FETISH BOOTS
Europe, c. 1900
Leather

M.2007.211.336A–B

When the top edge of the corset lowered, the breasts were left effectively unsupported. A boned camisole (or bust bodice) fit the silhouette of the monobosom, but after 1908 the emphasis on the breasts created by the Empire silhouette required a modified undergarment. Paul Poiret's delicate *brassière*, made from a single piece of fabric, for his wife and muse, Denise, was a variation of an earlier and more substantial model created for tennis and horseback riding.

Paul Poiret
France, 1879–1944
BRASSIÈRE, c. 1915
Cotton plain weave with cotton plain-weave appliqués
M.2007.211.980

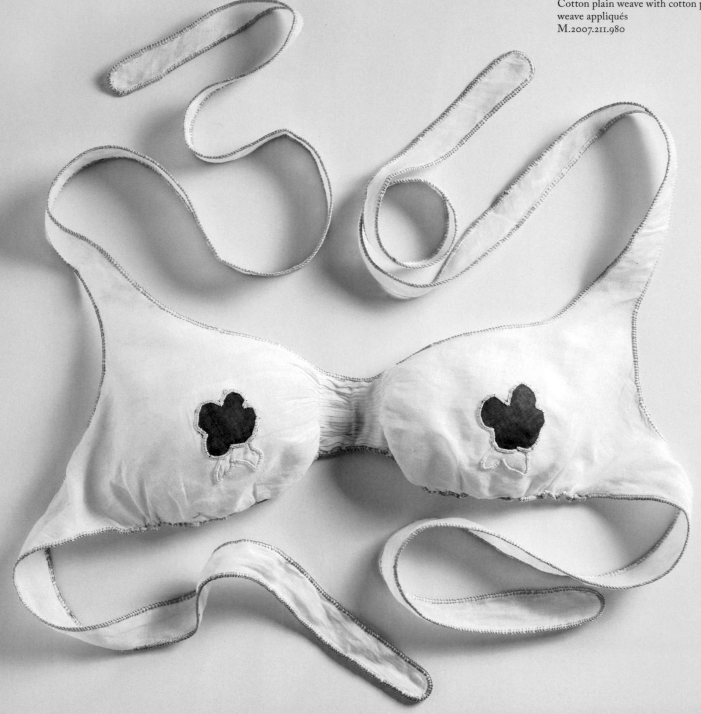

Trim

The disparate trim techniques found on fashionable dress were by and large unified by two humble objects: needle and thread—the tools necessary for embroidery, quilting, beading, and lacework. Although often perceived as mere icing on the cake, such finishing touches often represented the largest financial investment of an ensemble. An elaborately embroidered gold border on a man's formal suit usually cost much more than the materials and labor required to tailor the suit itself.

As there could be a great range in the quality of trimmings, there also was variety in the type of person who produced them. The most complex and costly embroidery projects were reserved for male guild members who had undergone extensive training and apprenticeships, though there also were other professional, semiskilled, and amateur embroiderers—both male and female—who worked in workshops or in their own homes. Royal embroiderer Charles Germain de Saint-Aubin, in his 1770 treatise *Art of the Embroiderer*, revealed details about the working lives of professionals in France, the center for European embroidery: "This is one of the trades in which women can earn the highest daily wages. They are paid ordinarily… four francs per ounce of [gold thread] used. This sum is increased in proportion with the amount of work to be done or when the materials are finer or more delicate. Men, however, are paid more—the sum depending on their degree of talent or competency. The day's work is from six in the morning to eight in the evening; for longer hours, workers are paid double."

When colonial activity and international trade increased during the eighteenth and nineteenth centuries, lavishly trimmed goods often were imported in great quantities from centers of skilled production in countries such as China, Japan, India, and Turkey. Once Europeans developed a taste for these imported items, they began to imitate materials and techniques, blending exotic fashions with their own. For example, the art of embroidering with a hooked needle was popular in India and Turkey long before it worked its way into European craft production by the 1760s (when it became known as tambour work). In this and other ways, the people and products of non-European countries shaped European fashion.

Of course, Europe had its own internal dynamics that could directly impact trends for costly decorative trimmings. Centers for embroidery and lace production throughout France were nearly decimated during the French Revolution, as their niche market, aristocrats, suffered economic losses or fled the country. Many French artisans also left; those who remained survived with commissions from other European courts and held out for better days, which some experienced under Napoléon's regime. Throughout the nineteenth century, the rise and fall of empires directly influenced whether the ranks of skilled workers expanded or diminished. During hard times, many craftspeople migrated into related but less skilled forms of production. In addition, over the course of the nineteenth century, the process of industrialization offered the consumer inexpensive options, such as textiles printed to look embroidered, and machine-made laces at a fraction of the cost of handmade varieties. These technological advancements posed stiff competition for artisans forced to adapt to a changing world—and its changing fashions.

In the eighteenth century, highly talented embroiderers embellished fine ecclesiastical textiles as well as fashionable dress and furnishings using similar styles and techniques. Working costly metallic threads over vellum segments (*guipure*) and interlacing others in a "basket weave" (*gaufrure*), as seen on this altar frontal, required minute attention to detail and an exacting and skillful hand.

ALTAR FRONTAL
France or Italy, 1730–40
Silk satin with silk and metallic-thread embroidery
Gift of St. Edmund's Episcopal Church, San Marino, California
M.2009.76

Mantua (Court Dress)
England, c. 1740–45.
Embroidered silk with
silver thread
Victoria and Albert
Museum, London

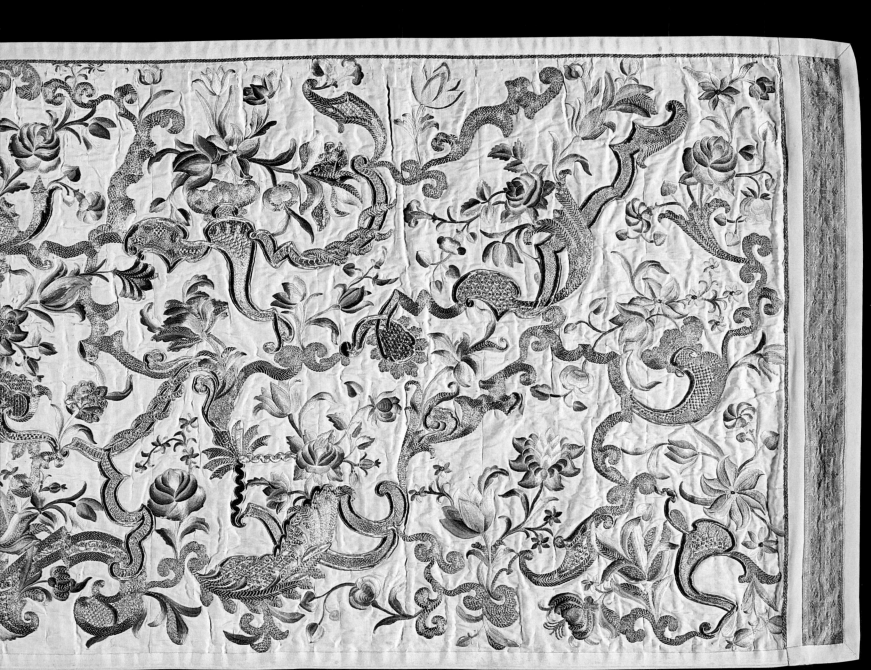

Men's at-home caps were worn as part of undress and had the practical purpose of keeping one warm in drafty houses. At-home caps also could be vehicles for displaying wealth and taste—particularly by virtue of the rich embroidery and lace trim that often adorned them. The high quantity of metallic thread suggests that these examples were professionally embroidered.

MAN'S AT-HOME CAP
Europe, 1700–1750
Silk plain weave with silk and metallic-thread embroidery, and metallic-thread lace trim
M.2007.211.826

MAN'S AT-HOME CAP
Switzerland, 1725–50
Silk plain weave with silk and metallic-thread embroidery, and metallic-thread lace trim
Costume Council Fund
M.81.97.12

MAN'S AT-HOME CAP
Probably France, 1725–75
Silk plain weave with supplementary warp-float patterning, and silk and metallic-thread embroidery
Gift of Mrs. Frederick Kingston
M.61.6

This velvet three-piece suit features embroidered floral motifs worked primarily in satin stitch. In select areas, stiff padding under the embroidery stitches creates added dimension, as is seen in the center of the dandelions. The velvet ground may have dictated, at least in part, the use of padding: embroiderers often employed vellum underlays when working on velvet in order to prevent fine stitches from sinking into the pile.

SUIT
Europe, c. 1800
Silk cut and voided velvet on plain-weave foundation with supplementary weft-float patterning and silk embroidery
Purchased with funds provided by Mr. and Mrs. John Jewett Garland
M.63.51A–C

Embroidered waistcoats became fashionable in the late eighteenth century as the suit narrowed and the coat curved away to reveal more of the waistcoat. This uncut-waistcoat panel is embellished with tambour embroidery (worked with a hooked needle) that illustrates the life cycle of a rose: bud, half bloom, and full bloom. A customer might examine a number of embroidered panels before selecting one to be tailored to his measurements.

UNCUT WAISTCOAT
France, c. 1760
Silk satin with silk embroidery

M.2007.211.814

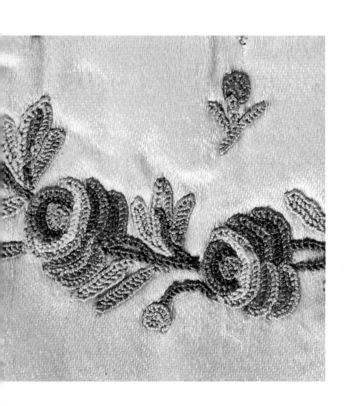

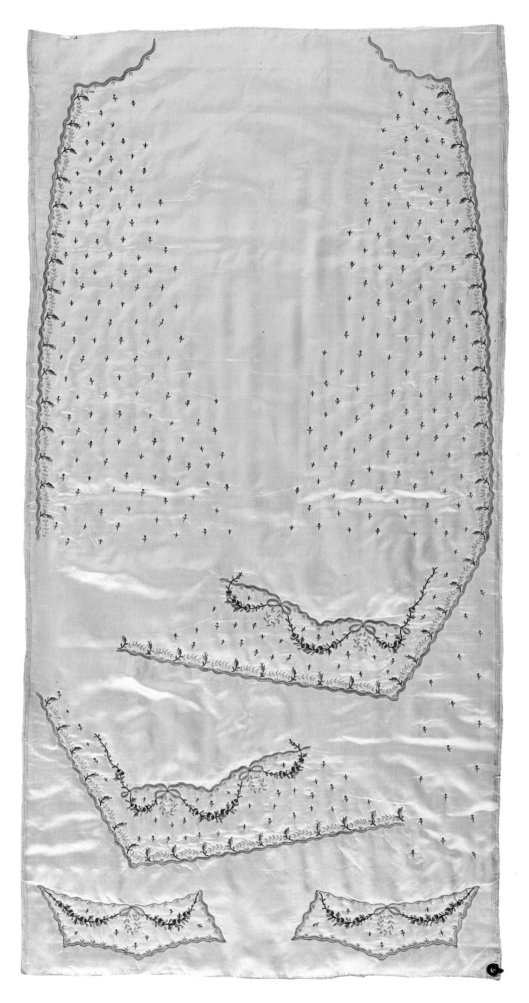

In the late eighteenth century, waistcoats continued to develop in importance; as they decreased in length, they were more commonly called vests. Men often owned dozens of vests that could be worn interchangeably with multiple suits. On this vest, silk floss in a range of colors is worked in delicate satin stitch to "paint" a pastoral scene.

VEST
France, c. 1785, altered c. 1795
Silk satin with silk embroidery and silk grosgrain ribbon
M.2007.211.1071

Playful attempts to "fool the eye" appealed to eighteenth-century sensibilities. On this vest, a cotton ribbon printed with rosebuds and speckles trims the garment, and below each pocket, embroidered green spots mimic the speckle motif, blurring the line between printing and embroidery. Visual artifice appears in the realistic tamboured "tassels" along the front, a common conceit of the period.

VEST
England, c. 1790
Cotton plain weave and twill with silk and metallic-thread embroidery and printed-cotton plain-weave trim
Costume Council Fund

M.63.54.3

Mitts were less restricting than gloves but still protected hands and forearms from the elements. The silk embroidery thread was once a vibrant golden hue. Yellow embroidery on off-white fabric was popular in Europe during the early eighteenth century; this style was influenced by traditional embroideries from Bengal, India, which featured naturally yellow tussar silk.

PAIR OF MITTS
England or India for the Western market, 1700–1725
Linen plain weave with silk embroidery
Costume Council Fund

M.80.43.4A–B

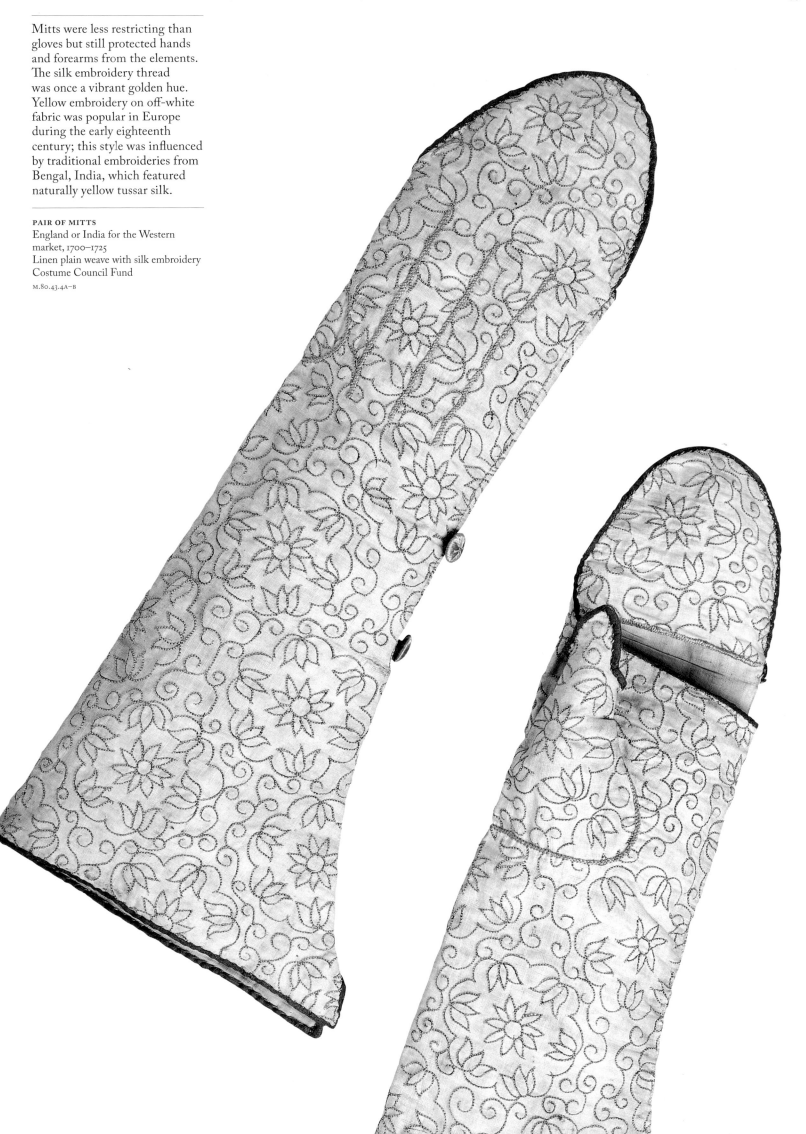

Elite women wore dress aprons
as a symbolic expression of
domesticity rather than as a
protective work garment. This
is one such example, with its
impractical white color and
delicate silk and metallic-
thread embroidery. The
apron may have been made
at home and incorporates
a technique known as
"pulled threadwork,"
which produces an
openwork pattern.

APRON
England, 1750–85
Cotton plain weave
with silk and
metallic-thread
embroidery
M.2007.211.131

PETTICOAT
England,
c. 1760
Silk satin,
quilted
Gift of Mrs.
Henry
Salvatori
M.79.19.2

An embroidered lattice background imparts structure to the scrolling vine motif that appears to meander freely across this bodice front (which originally may have been a woman's at-home waistcoat); however, the vines actually are highly symmetrical, each panel reflecting a mirror image of the other and different only in terms of color. Attracted to the greenery, a tiny caterpillar creeps along the bodice's lower right border.

BODICE FRONT
England or India for the Western market, 1730–60
Linen plain weave with silk and metallic-thread embroidery
M.2007.211.840

This *robe à la française* is embroidered with wool threads, prized for their vibrant dyed colors and practical ability to withstand washing. In the seventeenth century, when wool embroidery, or crewel work, enjoyed its first wave of popularity, it was applied primarily to home furnishings like curtains and bedcoverings rather than to clothes. By the early eighteenth century, crewel work appeared more frequently on fashionable dress.

**DRESS AND PETTICOAT
(ROBE À LA FRANÇAISE)**
France, textile c. 1750, constructed
c. 1760
Linen plain weave with wool embroidery
Gift of Dorothy Collins Brown in honor of the museum's 25th anniversary
M.90.83A–B

HAT (BERGÈRE)
England, 1750–60
Straw and silk satin with silk supplementary weft-float patterning
Costume Council Fund
M.64.85.3

PAIR OF ENGAGEANTES
Probably England, c. 1760
Cotton plain weave with cotton embroidery
Gift of Mrs. Henry Salvatori
M.79.19.6A–B

PAIR OF GLOVES
Europe, c. 1770
Cotton knit with cotton embroidery
M.2007.211.154A–B

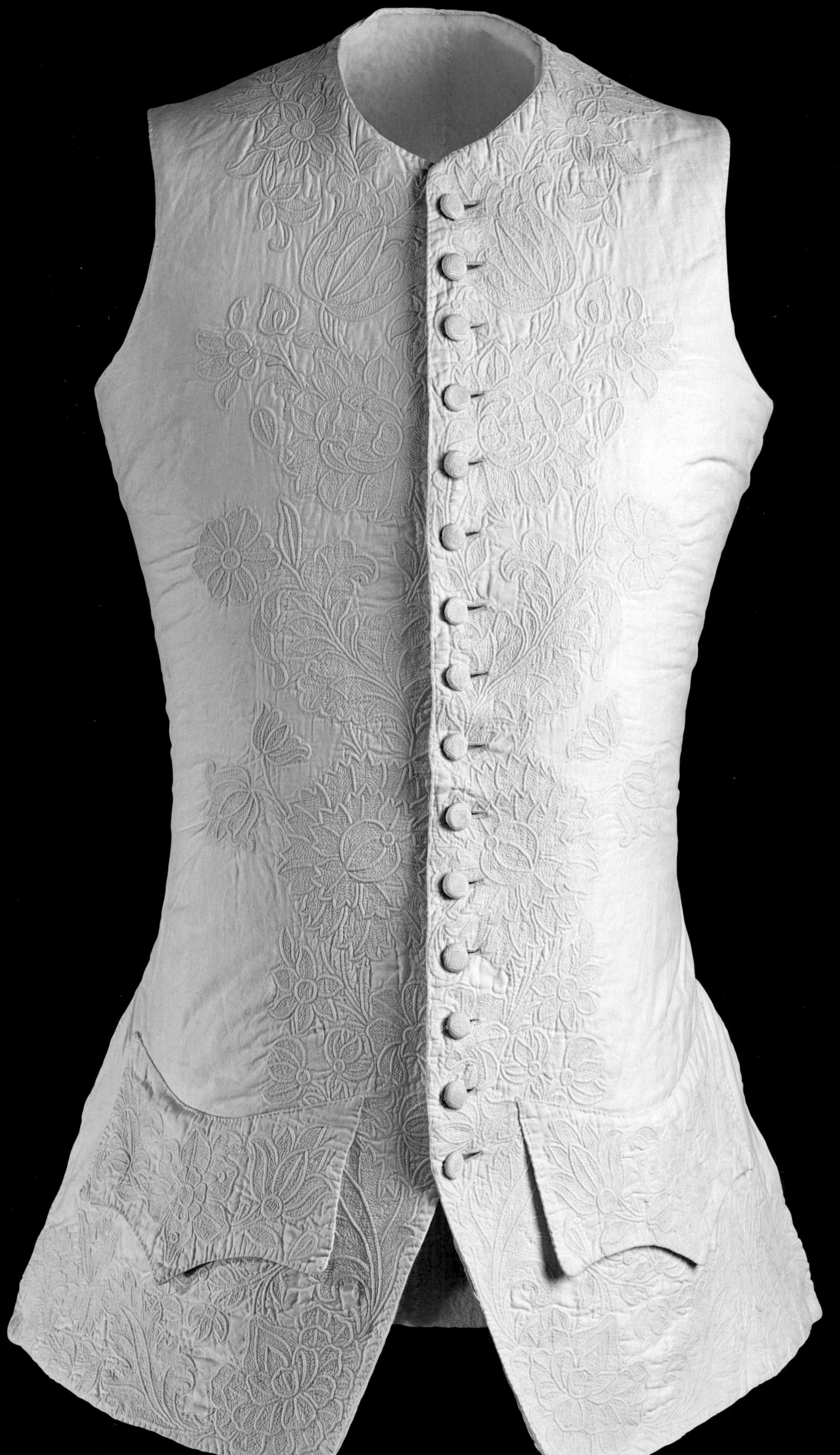

In corded quilting, motifs are outlined in parallel stitches that form channels on a fine fabric lined with a loosely woven piece of cloth. The quilter then uses a blunt needle to separate the warp and weft of the backing, inserting cord or yarn between the channels to create a raised pattern on the surface. Also known as Marseilles embroidery because of the superior quality of Provençal handwork, this technique can feature areas pebbled with miniature knots as well.

WAISTCOAT
Probably England, c. 1760
Cotton plain weave with cotton corded quilting
M.2007.211.813

STOMACHER
The Netherlands, 1740–50
Cotton plain weave with cotton embroidery and cotton corded quilting
Mrs. Alice F. Schott Bequest
M.67.8.98

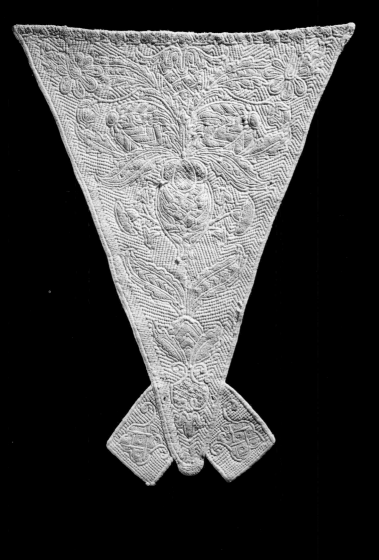

Exquisitely embroidered vignettes of chinoiserie figures on this petticoat eclipse the complexity of the quilted background. Symmetrical floral motifs define the upper register; in the lower register, however, free-form quilting stitches isolate and highlight the people and plants, while scalloped lines radiating from the figures echo the contours of the pink cartouches. Such intricate needlework seems incongruous for garments intended for informal or leisure wear.

PETTICOAT
Italy, 1725–60
Silk satin, quilted, with silk and metallic-thread embroidery
Costume Council Fund
M.59.27.1

A repeating pattern of flowers, including tiger lilies indigenous to Asia, has been embroidered across four panels of silk satin stitched together into a stylish petticoat. Each panel measures twenty-eight inches in selvage-to-selvage width, corresponding to the range of specified widths for silk fabrics ordered by the British East India Company. Completing this informal ensemble is a jacket, or caraco, made from a 1760s striped silk.

PETTICOAT
China for the Western market, c. 1785
Silk satin with silk embroidery
M.2007.211.708

JACKET (CARACO)
Europe, c. 1760, altered c. 1780
Silk plain weave with supplementary warp patterning
M.2007.211.3

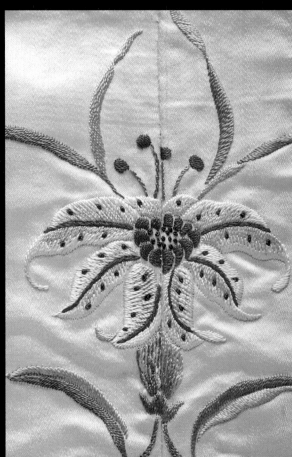

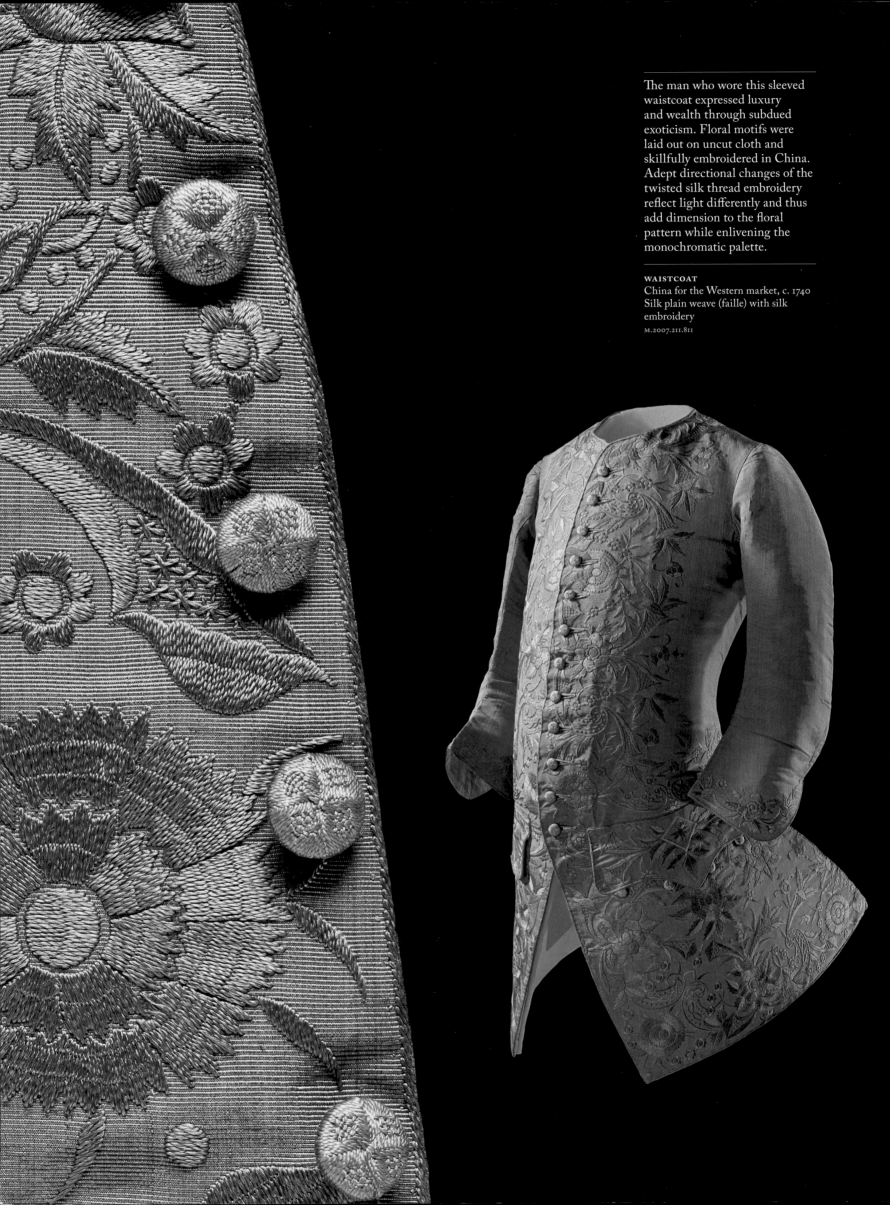

The man who wore this sleeved waistcoat expressed luxury and wealth through subdued exoticism. Floral motifs were laid out on uncut cloth and skillfully embroidered in China. Adept directional changes of the twisted silk thread embroidery reflect light differently and thus add dimension to the floral pattern while enlivening the monochromatic palette.

WAISTCOAT
China for the Western market, c. 1740
Silk plain weave (faille) with silk embroidery
M.2007.211.811

This English boy's frock is made of soft, lightweight cashmere twill woven in Kashmir. Prior to being cut and sewn, professional Indian embroiderers utilizing silk embroidery thread, probably imported from China, embellished the fabric with traditional stylized floral motifs that featured curved tips (*buta*) often seen on Kashmir shawls.

BOY'S FROCK
Kashmir, India, for the
Western market, c. 1855
Goat-fleece underdown (cashmere wool) twill with silk embroidery and silk tassels
M.2007.211.88

In the mid-nineteenth century, the insatiable demand in Europe for cashmere shawls created a design dialogue between East and West. Kashmir designs influenced "imitation Oriental shawls" manufactured in Europe, while new European designs were given to weavers in India to produce for the Western market.

This cashmere shawl is composed of multiple pieces of twill tapestry adeptly stitched together to create large, sweeping designs similar to those found on shawls woven on Jacquard looms in Europe.

SHAWL
Kashmir, India, mid-19th century
Goat-fleece underdown (cashmere wool) twill with double-interlocking tapestry-weave patterning, pieced, with wool embroidery
Gift of Anna Bing Arnold
60.46.12

This French version of the cashmere shawl was woven on a Jacquard loom, which employed a punch card system that directed the pattern sequence. The Jacquard loom enabled the creation of increasingly elaborate motifs with an expanded use of colors, thus producing shawls at a fast, economical rate. Wool wrapped around a silk core was utilized in an attempt to simulate the finest qualities of the much desired featherweight cashmere wool.

SHAWL WITH PRESENTATION BOX
Paris, 1860–70
Shawl: wool and silk twill with supplementary weft patterning; presentation box: paper-covered cardboard
M.2007.211.203A–B
Label: COMPAGNIE DES INDES. / CACHEMIRES-DENTELLES.

In the nineteenth century, Westerners were captivated by the exotic Japanese kimono but found the long, trailing robe impractical to wear. This imported "kimono" dressing gown, embellished with Japanese maple leaves tinged with autumnal colors and embroidered with the name "Emmie" on the left front, was cut shorter than a traditional kimono, tailored with additional side gores to accommodate a Western woman's wider gait, and included a soft Western-style sash with knotted fringe.

DRESSING GOWN
Japan for the Western market, c. 1885
Gown: silk crepe with silk embroidery; sash: silk plain weave with silk embroidery and knotted fringe
M.2007.211.783A–B

CORSET
England, c. 1890
Cotton plain weave with silk embroidery, linen lace with silk satin ribbon trim, and metal
M.2007.211.362

CHEMISE
Russia, c. 1890
Linen plain weave with linen lace
M.2007.211.438

Padded silk dressing gowns were produced in Japan for the Western market after the Japanese government sent a Yokohama silk merchant to the 1873 Vienna International Exposition to conduct market research on possible new export items. These dressing gowns followed European fashion in cut but often were embroidered with Japanese motifs such as this bird-and-flower design—focusing attention on the front of the garment as opposed to the back, which was traditionally the case with the Japanese kimono.

DRESSING GOWN
Yokohama, Japan, for the Western market, c. 1885
Gown: silk plain weave (faille) with silk embroidery; belt: silk braided cord with tassels
M.2007.211.784A–B

From the late eighteenth century, there was a concern that children's clothing should promote health and ease of movement. This resulted in a somewhat uniform ensemble for girls and boys consisting of a gown and pantalettes, preferably of cotton. This infant girl's dress is embroidered with a sprigged design inspired by Indian and Turkish textiles. Another nod to the "exotic" is found in the embroidered palms at the hem.

GIRL'S DRESS
Europe, c. 1805
Cotton plain weave (muslin) with cotton embroidery and cotton passementerie
M.2007.211.81

This boy's frock incorporates a white-work technique, *broderie anglaise*, in which small eyelets are outlined with sturdy embroidery stitches and cut out of the ground fabric. Although the result resembled lace, it could withstand frequent washing and was therefore practical for children's clothing. Technically very simple, this "imitation lace" was lower in cost than real lace, and it became increasingly available as the nineteenth century progressed. Ironically, this "democratic" decoration owed its affordability to the meager wages given to the female and child laborers who often produced it.

BOY'S FROCK
Probably England, c. 1855
Cotton plain weave with cotton cutwork embroidery (*broderie anglaise*)
M.2007.211.89

A domestic craft since the late sixteenth century, needlepoint became more standardized in 1804 when a Berlin publisher mass-produced graphed patterns that clearly indicated the color for each stitch. Berlin work, as it came to be known, featured vibrant wool yarns and complicated stitch techniques, which often were stored for future reference on samplers. This sampler measures approximately fifty by eight inches, and includes materials (silk, glass beads, imitation pearls) and techniques (note the black "lace" segment) newly incorporated into the craft around the 1860s.

SAMPLER
England, c. 1860
Linen canvas with wool, silk, and metallic-thread needlepoint, and glass and metallic beads (Berlin work)
Costume Council Fund
M.2009.50

Berlin work patterns were sold in shops and included in women's magazines to be stitched up by ladies at home. Note how the lapel on this vest panel was worked on the reverse side of the canvas ground so that the front of the needlework would be revealed when the lapel was turned back.

UNCUT VEST (DETAIL)
England, c. 1855
Cotton canvas with wool needlepoint (Berlin work)
M.2C07.211.824A–B

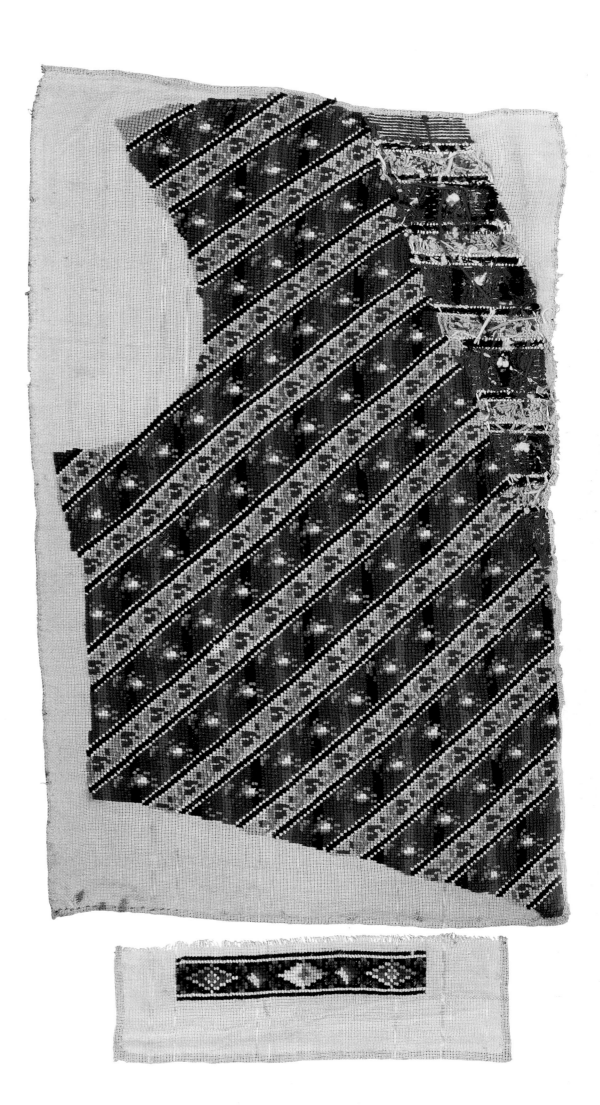

The programmatic method of Berlin work changed the relationship between the domestic embroiderer and her products: her role in design and the potential for improvisation diminished. At the same time, the straightforward process attracted many newcomers to needlepoint as a domestic pastime.

PURSE
Europe, c. 1840
Cotton canvas with wool needlepoint (Berlin work), silk-braided cord, and silk-chenille tassels
M.2007.211.280

Throughout most of the nineteenth century, women transformed interiors and fashionable accessories as they meticulously made up Berlin work slippers, tea cozies, fire screens, and purses. The assistance of a cobbler would have been required to complete these leather-soled slippers.

PAIR OF BOY'S SLIPPERS
Europe, 1800–1850
Cotton canvas with wool needlepoint (Berlin work), wool plain weave, silk plain weave, and leather
M.2007.211.309A–B

PAIR OF MAN'S SLIPPERS
Europe or United States, 1850–1900
Linen canvas with wool needlepoint (Berlin work), and leather
Mrs. Alice F. Schott Bequest
M.67.8.165A–B

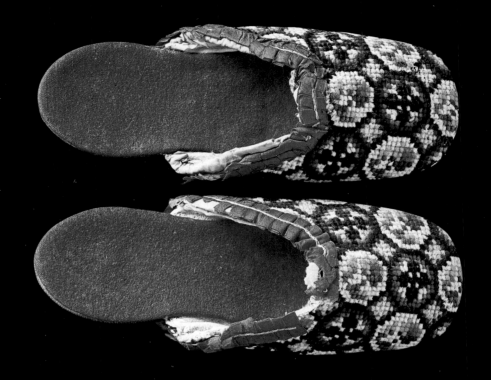

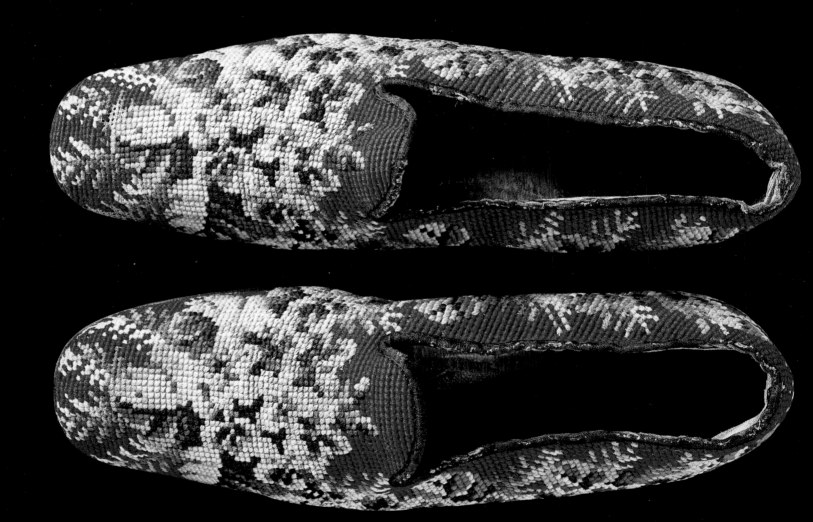

VEST
France, 1789–94
Linen canvas with silk needlepoint,
linen plain weave with silk
supplementary-warp cut-pile trim and
silk embroidery
M.2007.211.1078

Revolutionary Vest

ON JULY 14, 1789, AN ANGRY MOB STORMED the Bastille prison in Paris. It was the catalyst that transformed a long-simmering spirit of revolt against the French monarchy into a violent revolution. The leaders of the new regime took pride in wearing informal, even slovenly dress, and those who did not follow their example lived in fear of persecution.

Though the French Revolution would have devastating consequences for the Paris fashion industry, it was a fertile period for fashion itself, as clothing became a canvas for intense political debates. Fashion did not just take inspiration from the Revolution but explicitly advertised political loyalties.

Vests were one of the first garments affected. In the second half of the eighteenth century, as the cut of men's coats changed to reveal more of the torso, their vests grew increasingly pictorial, depicting scenes from fables, plays, and fashionable life. "On some fat abdominal protuberances, one admires grape harvests, regiments of cavalry marching on parade, hunts with all their paraphernalia, and a thousand other episodes of life, according to the taste of the connoisseur."[17] In the volatile political climate of the time, the range of subject matter quickly expanded from personal predilections to current events.

After the fall of the Bastille, royalists wore vests "covered with fleurs-de-lis, their pockets full of pistols," ready to defend the king.[18] At the opposite end of the political spectrum, the radical politician Maximilien de Robespierre (1758–1794) owned a vest decorated with revolutionary figures and inscriptions.

This extremely rare example, ripe with Revolutionary symbolism, must have belonged to a noble convert to the cause; through his clothing, he renounced aristocratic finery and declared his allegiance (real or prudently feigned) to the strict sartorial principles of the Revolution. The most obvious sign of this allegiance is the vest's color scheme. Blue and red were the colors of the flag of the city of Paris; white represented the French monarchy. Together, they were adopted as the colors of the Revolution (and, later, the French flag). Those loyal to the Revolution—male and female—sported tricolor cockades, ribbons, textiles, and accessories.

Although it appears to be knitted, the vest is actually done in petit point, a needlepoint stitch done on canvas. The superficial resemblance to knitting is surely deliberate, however; the *tricoteuses* (female professional knitters) of Paris were early and vocal supporters of the Revolution, and the vest claims kinship with these patriotic, working-class women.

The mottoes and motifs embroidered on the vest may seem enigmatic, but they had clear and specific meanings. In the 1780s, for a man to appear *en chenille* (as a caterpillar) was slang for being casually dressed; in the evening, he would metamorphose into a colorful, flamboyant "butterfly."[19] But the Revolution made such flamboyance politically incorrect, and here the metaphor is twisted in service of ideology. On the vest's left lapel, an airborne butterfly has its colorful wings clipped by an enormous pair of scissors. On the right, we see the newly shorn caterpillar brought down to earth, his unadorned body

now dwarfing the wings and scissors lying discarded on the green grass. The message, which would have been obvious to contemporaries, is that the former butterfly has sacrificed his finery, literally as well as figuratively, because an old vest of luxurious striped green silk has been repurposed as a lining for this vest. Because green was the color of the livery worn by servants of the Comte d'Artois, brother to King Louis XVI, it was considered a counter-revolutionary hue.

On the vest's pockets are familiar French sayings. On the right pocket is the phrase "L'HABIT NE FAIT PAS LE MOINE" ("The habit does not make the monk") which is roughly equivalent to the English idiom, "Don't judge a book by its cover," and may also refer to the Revolutionary government's dismantling of the Catholic Church. On the other pocket is stitched "HONI SOIT QUI MAL Y PENSE," medieval French for: "Shame upon him who thinks evil of it." While the sense of the latter phrase is similar to that of the former, it also carries a political subtext, for it was the motto of the Order of the Garter, England's oldest and most prestigious order of chivalry. England was a constitutional monarchy, and English politics and pastimes (like drinking tea and horse racing) became wildly popular in France in the decade leading up to the Revolution. French fashion, too, took inspiration from England's characteristic hats, jackets, and riding coats. On the eve of the Revolution, the American envoy to France observed in a letter to the newly elected president George Washington: "Everything is *à l'anglaise*, and a desire to imitate the English prevails alike in the cut of a coat, and the form of a constitution."[20]

The word "CHARMANT" (charming) stitched twice around the vest's collar is not just a playful boast; it also calls attention to the new fashion for cropped, unpowdered hair among supporters of the Revolution, an expression of the general fascination with the democratic politics and austere aesthetics of classical antiquity. On November 15, 1790, the fashion magazine *Journal de la mode et du goût* reported that young men dressed with "the greatest simplicity" and wore their hair "cut and curled like that of an antique bust." The style was dubbed *à la Titus* the following spring, when the actor François-Joseph Talma (1732–1799) adopted it to play Titus in a production of Voltaire's Roman tragedy *Brutus*. Revolutionary dress owed as much to ancient Greece and Rome as it did to England.

Though he declared himself to be a mere caterpillar, the wearer of this extraordinary garment clearly retained some of his butterfly's panache. Obviously, a great deal of time and thought went into the creation of this vest; it is difficult to believe that the wearer was wholly indifferent to fashion and finery. Flaunting his Revolutionary colors while protesting that clothes don't make the man, he wore his politics on his sleeve even as he distanced himself from them. The vest gives us a snapshot of a man—and a nation—undergoing a butterflylike transformation but, for the moment, still having it both ways.

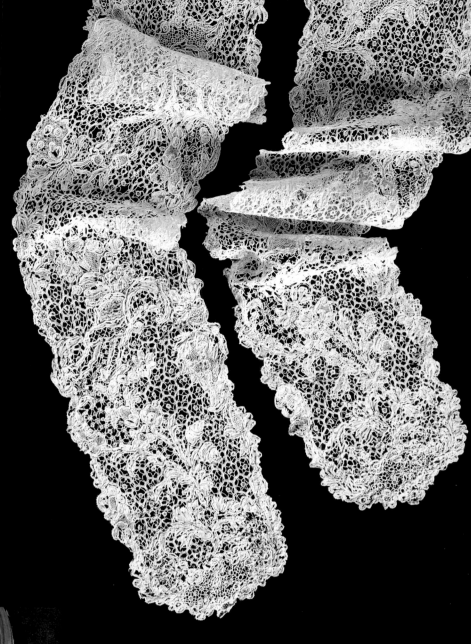

In the eighteenth century, men's lace accessories included cuffs, shirt ruffles, and neckties called cravats. Such fine handmade accessories were extremely costly additions to formal dress. This cravat of delicate point d'Alençon, a French needle lace, would have been attached to a linen band that could be removed as needed for cleaning or replacement.

CRAVAT (DETAIL)
France, c. 1795
Linen lace
Purchased with funds provided by
Mr. and Mrs. John Jewett Garland
M.63.15.3

Alexis Simon Belle
Portrait of Louis XV on His Throne Dressed in His Coronation Robes
(detail), 1723
Oil on canvas
Châteaux de Versailles et de Trianon, Versailles, France

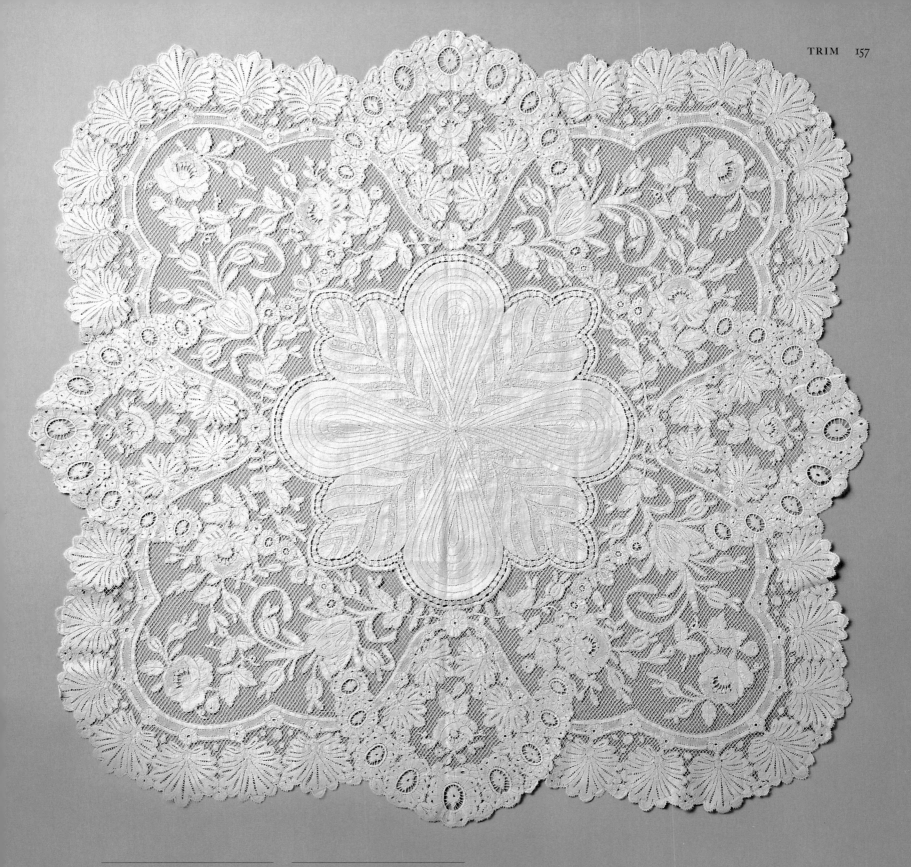

Decorative streamers known as lappets were important components of women's headdresses throughout much of the eighteenth century. This example represents a very fine and rare form of handmade French needle lace known as Argentella, a variation of point d'Argentan lace, characterized by tiny hexagons within hexagons.

LAPPETS (DETAIL)
France, 1725–75
Linen lace
Gift of Miss Cora E. Sanders
60.39

By the late nineteenth century, quality machine-made laces had grown more sophisticated and difficult to distinguish from handcrafted varieties. This exquisite bobbin-lace handkerchief was a considerable extravagance given that it was handmade and meant to be seen rather than used.

HANDKERCHIEF
Ghent, Belgium, 1850–75
Linen plain weave with cotton lace
Costume Council Fund
M.87.236

This overdress is of handmade bobbin lace known as Bucks, so called for its place of manufacture in Buckinghamshire, England. From 1808 a machine-made version of bobbin lace was increasingly available and popular. Given that machine net was less expensive and had a similar appearance, the choice of handmade lace for this deceptively simple gown would have made sense only to an elite customer who put a premium on luxury handcrafted garments.

DRESS
England, c. 1818
Linen lace
Costume Council Fund
M.63.54.5

PAIR OF SHOES
United States, c. 1800
Leather with silk trim
M.2007.211.295A–B

Label: Jas. Ringwood / Ladies & Gentlemens / FASHIONABLE Boot & Shoe Maker / BRIDGNORTH

This dress is covered with a handmade lace with a characteristic knotted ground known as filet. Historically, filet was used in decorative furnishings throughout Renaissance Europe and experienced a revival in the late nineteenth century along with other handmade laces. Thus, its inclusion in high fashion, such as in this evening gown, is noteworthy. Belle Epoque couture houses like Callot Sœurs, Worth, and Doucet made liberal use of lace.

Attributed to Callot Sœurs
Paris, active 1895–1937

DRESS, 1910–15
Linen lace and silk satin with silk-knotted fringe
Gift of Mrs. Andre de Limur
54.110.8A–B

HAT
Paris, c. 1910
Horsehair, raffia, wire, and ostrich feathers
Gift of Bullock's
M.74.24.63
Label: Mme Maerie / IMPORTER / PARIS-CHICAGO

By the mid-nineteenth century, machine-made lace progressed in complexity and pattern beyond simple bobbin net. Newly improved technologies made possible a variety of lace trim and accessories, some of them quite large, such as shawls and parasol covers. From 1838, when open carriages became popular, the demand increased for parasols as protection from the sun.

PARASOL
Europe, c. 1865
Silk lace, silk plain weave (taffeta),
wood, and ivory
M.2007.211.160

Capes and mantelets were essential accessories for women's outdoor wear in the last decades of the nineteenth century. Although this mantelet is covered in a relatively simple machine lace, the delicately ruched silk chiffon lining and woven label confirm its status as a high-end luxury garment.

MANTELET
Paris, c. 1902
Cotton lace, silk chiffon, silk-velvet ribbon, and sequins
Gift of Mrs. William Randolph Hearst Jr.
59.68.9
Label: Henriette Favre / 5 Rue de la Paix 5

CAPE
Paris, c. 1895
Cotton lace, silk plain weave,
and gelatin sequins
Gift of Mrs. Ivan M. Wells
CR.76.57.1
Label: PARIS / Stamler & Jeanne /
43. Avenue de l'Opéra

A richly patterned machine lace decorates this bonnet. By the third quarter of the nineteenth century, machine laces had secured a dominant position in fashion. An excerpt from the February 1885 issue of *Myra's Journal* describes just how acceptable they had become: "Imitation laces are now so well made, and in such handsome patterns, that they are used in the same way [as real lace]."

BONNET
Paris, c. 1880
Cotton lace and plain weave with ostrich feathers, silk-velvet ribbon, sequins, metal, and paste stones
M.2007.211.660
Label: Mangin Maurice / 27. Rue du 4 Septembre / PARIS.

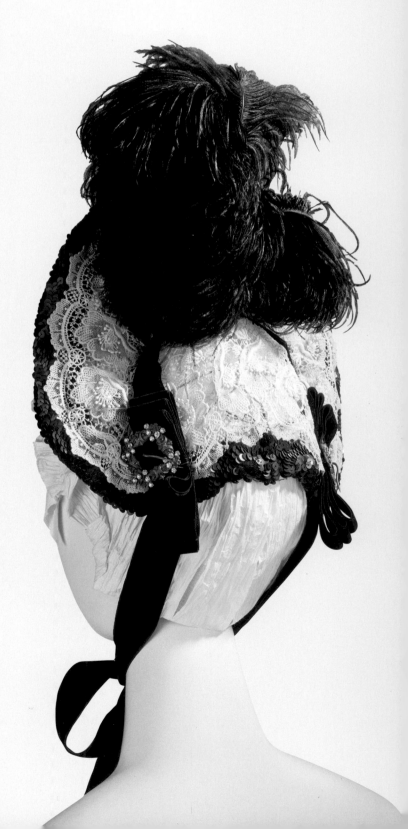

The use of decorative beadwork expanded substantially in the second half of the nineteenth century, when beads adorned everything from coats to chairs. The great demand for sparkling ornament came at a high price: in addition to the abuses suffered by bead workers in factories who worked fourteen-hour days in unhealthful conditions for negligible pay, women working at home on commission received paltry sums for their time-consuming, labor-intensive products for the wealthy.

BONNET
Probably France, 1880–85
Silk net with glass beads, ostrich feathers, leather tremblants, silk satin ribbons, and metal
M.2007.211.713

BONNET (FANCHON)
England, c. 1860
Linen net with lace, silk-velvet ribbon, and faux-pearl glass beads
M.2007.211.172

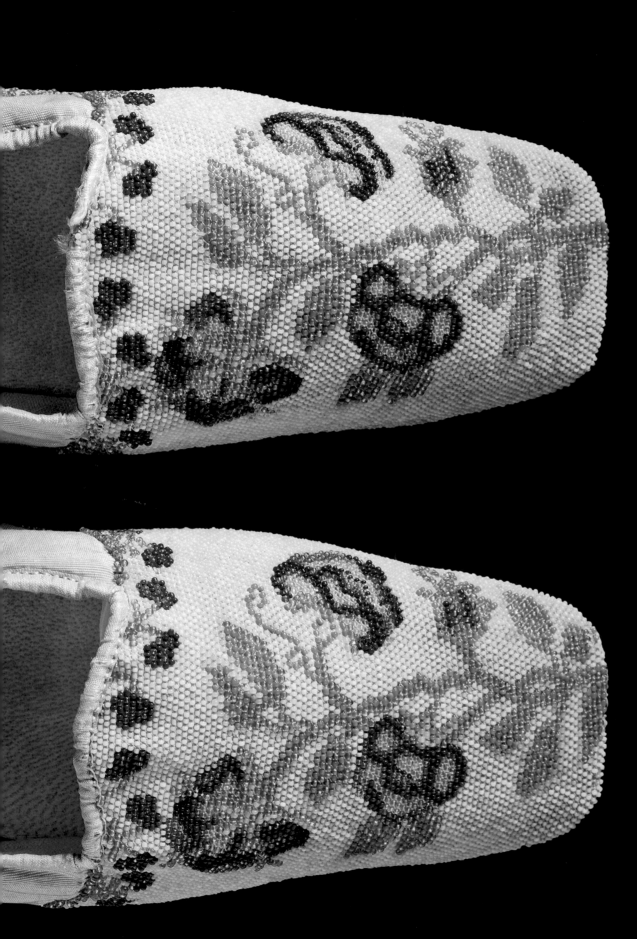

The simplicity of the neoclassical silhouette required scaled-down accessories that remained fashionable until the 1850s; women sometimes carried very small purses called "ridicules" (later reticule) in mockery of the bag's impracticality, and tiny parasols, more decorative than functional. Beaded accessories featured scenes or symbols of Romanticism: tombstones and weeping figures to illustrate love and death (p. 169 top); myriad flowers and foliage for harmony with nature; and the pinecone-shaped Indian *buta* for pre-occupation with the foreign and "exotic" (pp. 170–171). For men, small pouches for storing tobacco were decorated with attributes of masculine pursuits—hunting, drinking, and gambling (p. 169 bottom). Long, tubular "miser" (also called stocking or wallet) purses, worn over the belt by men and women, were shaped asymmetrically to separate and identify coins placed at either end (p. 168 right).

PAIR OF SHOES
Europe, 1840–55
Silk plain weave with glass beads, and leather
M.2007.211.348A–B

BAG (RETICULE)
England, c. 1840
Silk plain weave with silk needlepoint, glass- and metallic-bead embroidery, and metallic cord and fringe
M.2007.211.270

168

BAG (RETICULE)
Europe, c. 1810
Silk knit with glass beads and silk cord
M.2007.211.248

MAN'S TOBACCO POUCH
Probably England, 1820–30
Silk knit with glass and metallic beads,
and leather lining
Anonymous gift
M.85.240.76

PARASOL
Europe, c. 1805
Silk knit with glass and steel beads,
wood, bone, and metal
Mrs. Alice F. Schott Bequest
M.67.8.123

BAG (RETICULE)
France, 1810–20
Silk knit with glass beads, metal-hinged
clasp, and metal chain
M.2007.211.260

PARASOL
England, c. 1840
Silk knit with glass beads, wood, bone,
and metal
M.2007.211.158

BAG (RETICULE)
Europe, c. 1830
Silk knit with glass and metallic beads
M.2007.211.267

In the early 1880s, the bustle took the form of a horizontal shelf at the back of the waist, from which the skirt hung straight down. Bustled gowns were designed to be equally attractive from the front and back. Here, the large, elaborate knotted tassel at the back of the bodice is clearly intended to call attention to the bustle.

DRESS
France, c. 1885
Silk plain weave (taffeta) and silk plain weave with warp-float patterning and supplementary weft, and silk knotted tassel
M.2007.211.34A–B

BAG (RETICULE)
France, c. 1799
Silk satin with weft-float and supplementary weft-float patterning, silk floss and chenille passementerie with silk fly fringe, and silk cord
Gift of Mr. and Mrs. Robert D. Mathey
M.83.281.2

Fly fringe was a form of braid or tassel consisting of a cord ornamented with silk floss knotted into tufts. Here, the fluttering three-dimensional trim adds movement and texture to an already ornate fabric—a silk faille with woven polychrome flowers and moiré (watered) finish. While many ladies made fly fringe as a hobby, this perfectly color-coordinated union of textile and trimming suggests a sophisticated professional collaboration between weaver, braid maker, and fabric dealer.

DRESS (ROBE À LA FRANÇAISE)
Probably the Netherlands, c. 1775
Silk plain weave (faille) with supplementary weft-float patterning, moiré finish, and silk passementerie with silk fly fringe
M.2007.211.926A–B

Paul Poiret's June 1911 party, "The Thousand and Second Night," a spectacle of brilliantly colored textiles, exotic fauna, and sumptuously costumed guests, was inspired by *The Arabian Nights*. This collection of tales of ancient Indian and Persian origin, translated at the time as *One Thousand and One Nights*, contributed to the French fascination with Orientalism. This turban epitomized the European conception of "Persian" dress and was worn by Poiret's wife, Denise, as the extravaganza's Queen of the Harem.

Paul Poiret
France, 1879–1944

TURBAN, 1911
Silk and metallic-thread plain weave, silk plain weave, turquoise cabochon, and egret feathers
M.2007.211.979

Denise and Paul Poiret at "The Thousand and Second Night" Party, 24 June 1911 (detail), 1911
Published in *Poiret: Paul Poiret 1879–1944*, by Yvonne Deslandres with Dorothée Lalanne, Rizzoli, 1987

The spectacular productions of the Ballets Russes in Paris, inspired by the brilliant hues, motifs, and styles of Asia, significantly influenced fashion in the second decade of the twentieth century. Couturiers such as Paul Poiret and the Callot sisters introduced glittering ornamentation, exotic feathers, turbans, and harem pants into the mode. A bifurcated garment in any style, even if long and voluminous, was considered a controversial innovation in fashionable dress because it challenged established gender roles.

Callot Sœurs
Paris, active 1895–1937

LOUNGING PAJAMAS, C. 1913
Silk net (tulle) and silk satin (charmeuse) with metallic-thread passementerie and silk tassels
Gift of Alexander J. and Anthony D. Cassatt
54.97.17A–B

PAIR OF SHOES
London, c. 1913
Silk satin with glass and metallic beads, plastic sequins, and leather
Wilma Alice Leithead Wood Bequest
58.34.43A–B

Label: HOOK KNOWLES / & CO. LD. / MAKERS TO THE / ROYAL FAMILY / 66 & 65 / NEW BOND ST / LONDON

Émile Pingat's eveningwear was distinguished by its inventive combination of contrasting materials. For this mantle, the couturier joined crisp wool, usually associated with daywear, with the shimmering softness of velvet as a pristine foil to the lavish concentration of ornament. A wealth of glistening beads and embroidery highlight the curvilinear art nouveau patterns.

Émile Pingat
France, active 1860–1896

MANTLE, c. 1891
Wool plain weave and silk velvet with silk and metallic-thread embroidery, glass beads, and ostrich-feather trim
M.2007.211.38

Freke Field
L'Attente (Waiting), 1890–94
Oil on canvas
Collection of Lynda and Stewart Resnick

In the eighteenth century, for formal occasions European men made liberal use of jewelry, including diamond or paste suit buttons. One set of costly buttons could be applied and detached as needed to accessorize multiple dress suits.

COAT AND WAISTCOAT (DETAIL)
Germany, c. 1805
Silk plain weave with supplementary warp- and weft-float patterning
M.2007.211.952A–B

SET OF COAT AND WAISTCOAT BUTTONS WITH CASE (DETAIL)
Germany, c. 1805
Paste stones set in gilt silver
M.2007.211.953A–RR

Bling

FOR MUCH OF THE EARLY MODERN PERIOD, the dominant economic theory throughout Europe was mercantilism. Many mercantilists believed that a nation's economic livelihood depended on a favorable balance of trade (exports should exceed imports) and the proper maintenance of wealth in the form of silver and gold bullion. These ideas impacted notions of the right way to dress, as well as how clothing might benefit—or harm—the health of the nation. Mercantilist author Thomas Mun (1571–1641) advised his English countrymen: "We may likewise diminish our importations, if we would soberly refrain from excessive consumption of forraign wares in our [clothing]... and if in our [clothing] we will be prodigal, yet let this be done with our own materials and manufactures, as Cloth, Lace, Imbroderies, Cutworks and the like."[21]

In addition to "buying local," within this framework it also made good economic sense to avoid "wasteful" use of scarce silver and gold, particularly with respect to fashion. In 1749 the English government even tried to ban metallic-thread embroidery, lace, and fringe on the grounds that such excessive use of precious resources threatened the national economy.

These ideals, however, rarely corresponded with reality. Just as European countries struggled to keep foreign cloth at bay, precious metals commonly adorned formal dress and accessories. These trimmings were extremely costly, literally worth their weight in silver and gold. Consequently, when a garment or its trim was no longer à la mode, it was common to unpick metallic components for resale and melting them down (a process called drizzling) so that costs could be recouped. It is therefore all the more remarkable that any garments survive with their precious-metal decor intact.

Working with costly trimmings demanded considerable skill and judgment on the part of the maker. At each step in the manufacturing process, artisans faced choices that impacted both practical and aesthetic concerns. Metallic-embroidery thread could twist easily or break or, worse yet, snag or cut the ground fabric. As for embroidery in sequins (paillettes), Charles Germain de Saint-Aubin (1721–1786), royal embroidery designer for Louis XV, had this to say in his 1770 treatise on embroidery, *Art of the Embroiderer*: "With the exception of the last paillette in each row, one only sees half of each paillette during the course of the work. The paillettes are placed like a fallen stack of coins. Those with economy in mind space the paillettes a little farther apart, which makes a difference [in cost] when dealing with a considerable quantity of paillettes. However, this work is less durable, and the outlines are less precise. The difference, nonetheless, sometimes adds up

to several ounces [of silver] when you have two workers embroidering identical pieces of work."[22] Clearly, artisans working with precious metals needed to strike a delicate balance between pleasing the eye and using expensive materials judiciously.

Lest we put too much stock in the charges of contemporary (male) authors that women's dress in particular threatened national economies, it is worth examining some of the glittering men's suits in closer detail to learn about male clothing fashioned with silver and gold. The embroidery on the chartreuse velvet court suit (pp. 17, 197) was done separately and then applied to the suit components. First, a pattern was drawn onto a plain piece of fabric that served as the foundation for the embroidery. Next, the sections that would remain hidden under the larger foil segments were worked with thick cotton thread in order to give the embroidery a three-dimensional effect. Then, the metal threads, foil, and sequins were sewn on according to the pattern. Once the embroidery was completed, the back of the fabric was stiffened with glue, the completed sections cut out, likely attached to paper, and rolled up to be readied for sale. Such premade trimmings shortened the delivery time for orders of richly embellished garments.

Around the close of the first decade of the nineteenth century, after several years of democratic simplicity in menswear, there was a return to formality and a renewed emphasis on surface decor in men's suits, particularly for court occasions. In some countries on the continent, the richly encrusted suit never really went away. But at Napoléon's court, French men had to reacquaint themselves with the discomfort of suits made extremely stiff and heavy by metallic embroidery, thick padding, and narrow tailoring, as seen in a red-wool court ensemble (pp. 198–201). Rather than couching—a method in which the metallic threads are "tacked on" to the front surface of the cloth—the silver embroidery is worked primarily in satin stitch. This method consumed a higher quantity of metallic thread than couching, and left much of the silver hidden on the back of the fabric. Although this technique required great skill in order to prevent snagging, threads worked in this way were much more secure than couched threads. Thus, embroiderers had to consider how to maximize the visual impact of the metallic threads without sacrificing the longevity of the garment. The following examples attest to the success they often achieved on both counts.

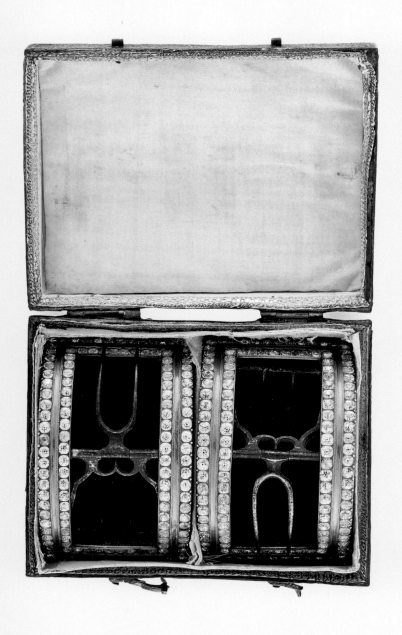

Once buckled shoes began to replace tied shoes in the late seventeenth century, glittering detachable buckles soon became de rigueur for formal occasions. A range of materials were used: brass, steel, and silver and silver gilt for the base, as well as diamonds, quartz, and glass or paste stones.

PAIR OF MAN'S SHOE BUCKLES WITH CASE
France, c. 1785
Paste stones with gilded-copper-alloy trim on silver and steel
M.2007.211.829A–C

PAIR OF MAN'S SHOE BUCKLES WITH CASE
France, 1785–90
Steel
M.2007.211.830A–C

PAIR OF SHOE BUCKLES
France, 1770–90
Metal and paste stones
M.2007.211.72A–B

PAIR OF MAN'S SHOE BUCKLES
France, c. 1785
Metal and paste stones
M.2007.211.71A–B

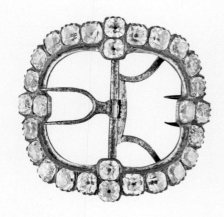

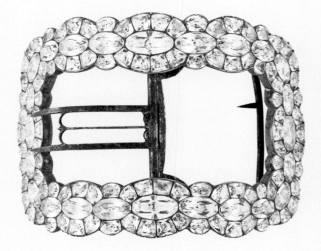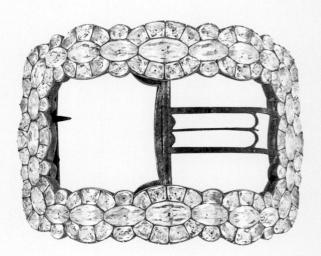

The metallic accents on painted and embroidered fans flickered as the owner fanned herself. Gold sequins on these examples were used in a painterly way to outline a cartouche or add pattern to a gown.

FAN
France, c. 1780
Silk plain weave, painted, with silk ribbon, sequins, and metallic-thread embroidery, and bone
Purchased with funds provided by Dr. and Mrs. Miguel A. Llanos
M.81.245.4

FAN (OVERALL AND DETAIL)
France, c. 1810
Paper, painted, with sequins and bone
Gift of Anita S. Watson
M.83.189.43A

Stomachers often served as decorative focal points for women's gowns, especially those created for formal or courtly occasions. When worn with a dress of silk and metallic threads, the stomacher can be seen as "jewelry" integral to the ensemble. Precious jewels, such as seed pearls, occasionally embellished formal stomachers. Women commonly attached jeweled brooches onto their elaborately decorated stomachers, creating a layered effect of riches upon riches.

STOMACHER
France, 1700–1750
Silk satin with metallic-thread lace, silk and metallic-thread plain-weave appliqués, metallic-thread passementerie, and tassels
Mrs. Alice F. Schott Bequest
M.67.8.99

STOMACHER (OVERALL AND DETAIL)
Probably Italy, 1725–75
Silk satin with silk and metallic-thread embroidery, sequins, seed pearls, and metallic-lace trim
M.2007.211.130

Louis Tocque (studio of)
The Queen of France Marie Leczinska
(detail), 1740
Oil on canvas
Châteaux de Versailles et de Trianon,
Versailles, France

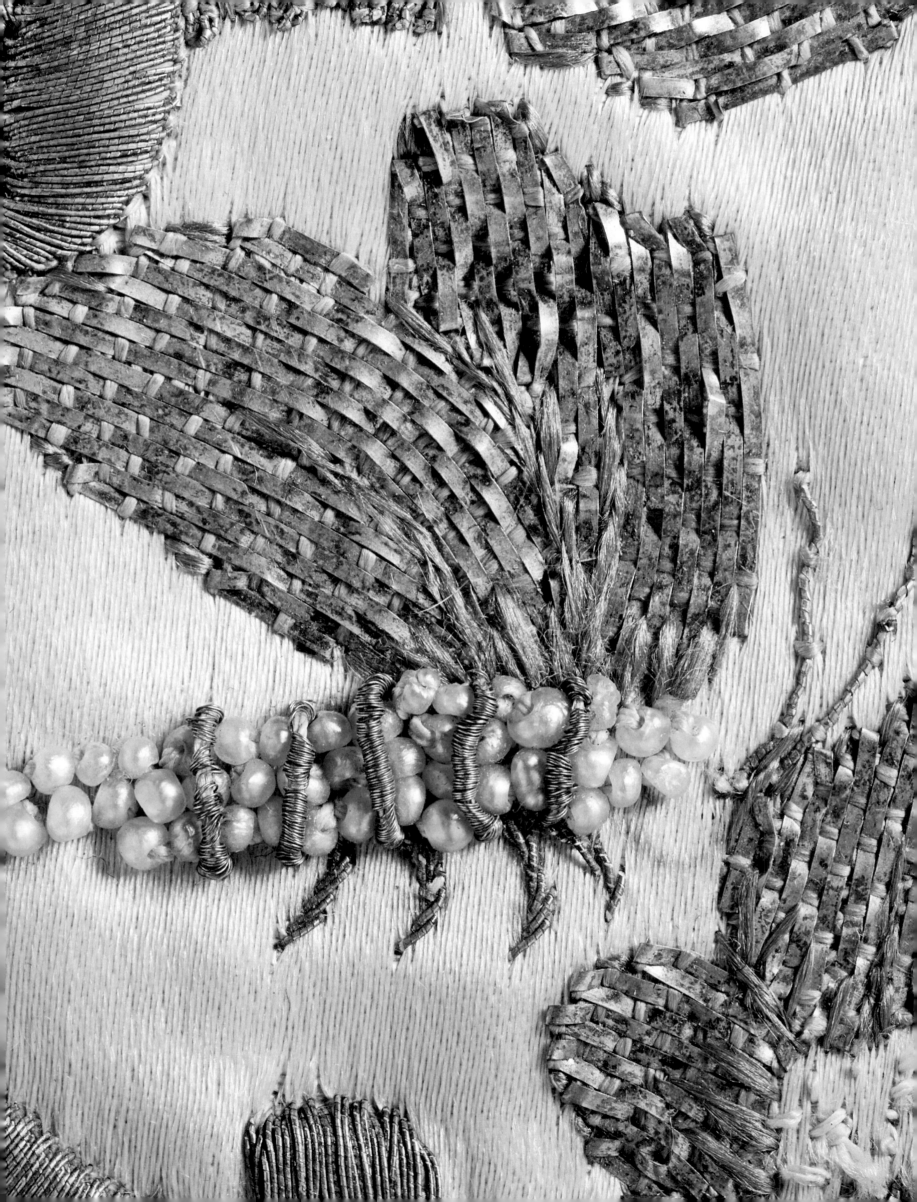

As fashionable dress obscured
women's legs completely, feet
and ankles were charged with
eroticism. Contemporary
accounts often convey men's
excitement when they caught a
furtive glance. A glimpse of the
embroidered silver bird alighting
just below the wearer's knee
would have been a titillating
sight.

**ONE OF A PAIR OF WOMAN'S
STOCKINGS**
Europe, 1700–1725
Silk knit with metallic-thread
embroidery

M.2007.211.134A–B

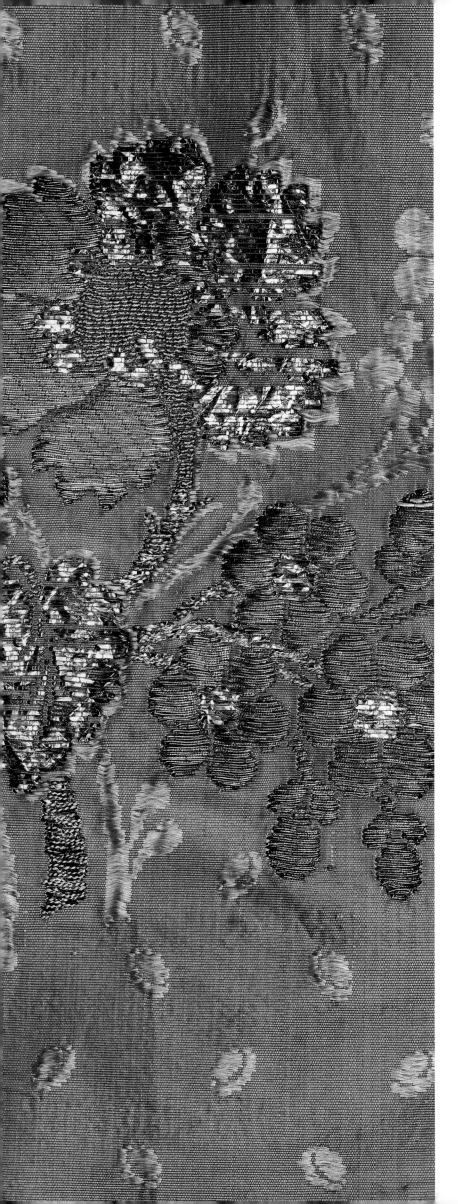

The silk textile of this formal gown is rendered especially complex with patterning that incorporates a range of silver threads: *lamella* (thread of flat metallic strips), *filé* (metallic thread wound on a silk core), and *frisé* (a silk and metallic spiraled thread). These variously textured threads catch and reflect light in different ways.

DRESS AND PETTICOAT
(ROBE À LA FRANÇAISE)
England, c. 1765
Silk plain weave (faille) with silk and metallic-thread supplementary-weft patterning, and metallic lace
M.2007.211.929A–B

This gown is frosted with pure silver bobbin lace. While the lace technique and pattern are relatively simple, any savings in its production would have been more than offset by the vast lengths of rich, costly materials that went into its creation.

DRESS AND PETTICOAT
(ROBE À LA FRANÇAISE)
England, c. 1760
Silk plain weave with weft-float patterning and silk with metallic-thread supplementary-weft patterning, and metallic lace
Gift of Mrs. Henry Salvatori
M.79.118A–B

STOMACHER
Probably England, mid-18th century
Silk satin with metallic-thread embroidery and passementerie
M.2007.211.129

The lavish embroidery on this suit consists of gold-coated silver threads and sequins. This stunning ensemble is remarkable for having survived the common practice of unpicking precious-metal trimmings. The wool fabric, a practical necessity during cold winter months, absorbs light in contrast to its reflective gilt trim. The suit weighs more than nine pounds.

SUIT
France, c. 1760
Coat and waistcoat: wool plain weave, full finish, with sequins and metallic-thread embroidered appliqués; breeches: wool plain weave, full finish, with silk and metallic-thread passementerie
M.2007.211.946A–C

The colorful embroidered trimmings appliquéd onto this suit incorporate green paste "gemstones," pink foil, and sequins. The owner chose the premade trim to coordinate with the coat's chartreuse velvet and pink satin lining. Completion of his opulent ensemble would have taken less time than a suit with embroidery worked directly into the garment's fabric.

SUIT
France, 1780–85
Coat and breeches: silk cut and uncut velvet on twill foundation with paste stones, foil, sequins, and metallic-thread embroidered appliqués; waistcoat: silk satin with foil, sequins, and metallic-thread embroidery
M.2007.211.950A–C

This wool coat and its companion cloth-of-silver vest are adorned with silver metallic-thread embroidery depicting naturalistic oak leaves and acorns interspersed amid stylized leaves. Embroidered directly onto the cloth in satin stitch, the heavily encrusted set weighs more than six and a half pounds. Its red wool lends a militaristic flavor to this court ensemble.

COAT AND VEST
Italy, c. 1810
Coat: wool plain weave, full finish, with metallic-thread embroidery; waistcoat: silk plain weave with metallic-thread supplementary weft, and metallic-thread embroidery
Costume Council Fund
M.80.60A–B

BREECHES
Italy, 1790–1810
Silk twill
Costume Council Fund
M.84.10.8

HAT (BICORNE)
France, c. 1790
Wool felt, beaver fur, ostrich feathers, and metallic passementerie
Mrs. Alice F. Schott Bequest
M.67.8.203

While neoclassicism dominated fashion after the French Revolution, it coexisted comfortably with a fascination with the exotic. If the color and silhouette of this gown were inspired by Classical statues, the silk-and-paillette-embroidered zigzag lines might be read as a reference to foreign lands: the "zebra stripe" was a popular textile motif in France in the late 1780s after King Louis XVI (1754–1793) acquired one of the unfamiliar animals. (See also p. 122.)

DRESS
Europe, textile 1785–90, dress c. 1795
Silk plain weave with weft-float patterning, silk and metallic-thread embroidery, sequins, silk and linen net, silk satin, and silk plain-weave (faille) trim
M.2007.211.933

PAIR OF SHOES
England, 1793–98
Silk satin with sequins and metallic passementerie, and leather
Costume Council Fund
M.59.24.29A–B

The shimmering palm-frond motifs throughout this gown are worked in satin stitch with metallic threads. As imperialistic programs in the nineteenth century intensified, more European women moved into colonial territories, where they were exposed to new modes of dress. Their receptivity stimulated the craze for "India muslins," turbans, fans, and exotic-plant motifs. In turn, these trends impacted European fashion and eventually found expression in the most formal court dress.

ENSEMBLE
Portugal, c. 1825
Dress: silk satin with silk, silk-chenille, and metallic-thread embroidery; hat: silk satin with metallic-thread embroidery; fan: silk satin and silk net with foil and sequins
M.2007.211.934A–C

Fit for a Queen

THIS GOWN IS A STUNNING EXAMPLE of mid-nineteenth-century court dress. It arrived at the Los Angeles County Museum of Art along with a fascinating story that it once belonged to Queen Maria II of Portugal (1819–1853), who gave it to a British naval officer, Sir George Sartorius (1790–1885), for having served on behalf of her father, Dom Pedro (1798–1834), and herself in the Portuguese civil war. In addition to its unique national identity and potential royal connection, the gown offers valuable insights into the construction of European court clothing in general and the customs associated with it in the mid-nineteenth century.

The bodice, skirt, and train are composed of black satin, a striking background to the golden embroidery that takes center stage. The embroidery threads consist of delicate strips of gilt copper, some of which have been textured during the manufacturing process. These are worked through the fabric in satin stitch, meaning much of this gold-plated thread lies hidden from view. Such materials and techniques demanded a highly skilled embroiderer, as the metallic threads could easily become twisted and/or cut the fabric. Dimension is added throughout the embroidered design with a padded underlay of thick cotton thread.

Generally speaking, European court dress followed the fashionable silhouette for eveningwear (even if court assembled in the daytime)—hence the full, gathered skirt and the wide lace collar known as a bertha, both popular in the mid-nineteenth century. But as court culture accepted only the most elite members of society, who were perceived as "a class apart" from everyone else, so did court attire possess some idiosyncratic characteristics that distinguished it from contemporary fashion. Most noteworthy for women's dress were the deep décolleté, short sleeves, and sweeping train. All once components of late-seventeenth-century fashion not specifically tied to court circles, by the late eighteenth century these features had become fossilized and persisted in courtly attire into the twentieth century. The train was the ultimate display of social power and material wealth: not only did it consume lengths of costly fabric and trim, but it also required the assistance of pages or ladies-in-waiting. This train lost at least fifteen inches at some point in the late nineteenth century, when the ensemble was altered for masquerade costume (a common practice of the time). Originally, it would have measured close to twelve feet long.

The choice for the color black in a formal court gown might seem austere to modern eyes and suggest the dress was worn for mourning. Certainly when a member of the royal family died, a period of deep mourning was officially decreed, and during such times black gowns were obligatory at court. However, black was a fashionable option for southern European court dress, and the elaborate gold embroidery would have made this example inappropriate during times of deep mourning. It is more likely that the dark color should be read as part of regional custom rather than somber dress code. This gown therefore blends local tradition with the dominant themes for court dress throughout Europe: formality, fossilization, and fashion.

DRESS AND TRAIN
Portugal, c. 1845;
Bodice: silk satin with metallic-thread
embroidery and silk net (tulle); skirt
and train: silk satin with metallic-
thread embroidery
M.2007.211.941A–B, D

Endnotes

FASHIONING (AND REFASHIONING) EUROPEAN FASHION

1 Louis-Sébastien Mercier, *Tableau de Paris*, ed. Jean-Claude Bonnet (Paris: Mercure de France, 1994), II.1194.

2 Ibid., I.1481.

3 Quoted in Marie J. Ghering van Ierlant, "Anglo-French Fashion, 1786," *Costume*, no. 17 (1983): 64.

4 *Transactions of the National Association for the Promotion of Social Science* (London: 1866), 495.

5 W. McIlwaine, *The Dress-maker* (London: Aylott and Jones, 1846), 22.

6 *Punch* (August 8, 1863): 59.

7 Mary Haweis, *The Art of Beauty* (Whitefish, Mont.: Kessinger Publishing, 2005), 36.

8 William Morris, "The Lesser Arts of Life," in Reginald Stuart Poole et al., *Lectures on art delivered in support of the Society for the Protection of Ancient Buildings* (London: Macmillan and Co., 1882): 221.

9 Oscar Wilde, *The Woman's World* (London: Cassell & Co., 1888), I.40.

10 Thorstein Veblen, *The Theory of the Leisure Class* (Boston: Houghton Mifflin, 1973), 69.

11 Quoted in Alice Mackrell, *Art and Fashion: The Impact of Art on Fashion and Fashion on Art* (London: B. T. Batsford, 2005), 95.

SEASIDE FASHION

12 *Punch* (July 31, 1850): 77.

13 Quoted in Avril Lansdell, *Seaside Fashions 1860–1939* (Princes Risborough, Buckinghamshire: Shire Publications, 1990), 17.

TENNIS DRESSING

14 Margaret Oliphant, *Dress* (London: Macmillan and Co., 1878), 87.

TALLYHO!

15 Frederick Peter Delmé Radcliffe, *The Noble Science: A Few General Ideas on Fox-hunting* (London: Rudolph Ackermann, 1839), 138.

16 R. S. Surtees, *Mr. Sponge's Sporting Tour* (London: Macmillan and Co., 1903), 31.

REVOLUTIONARY VEST

17 G. Touchard-Lafosse, *Chroniques de l'œil-de-boeuf* (Paris: Librairie Garnier Frères, 1926), V.467.

18 Madame de Chastenay, *Mémoires de Madame de Chastenay, 1771–1815*, ed. Alphonse Roserot (Paris: Librairie Plon, 1896), I.139.

19 Baron de Frénilly, *Mémoires de baron de Frénilly, 1768–1848. Souvenirs d'un ultra-royaliste*, ed. Frédéric d'Agay (Paris: Perrin, 1987), 36.

20 Gouverneur Morris, *The Diary and Letters of Gouverneur Morris*, ed. Anne Cary Morris (New York: Charles Scribner's Sons, 1888), I.31.

BLING

21 Thomas Mun, *England's Treasure by Forraign Trade* (1664), (New York and London: Macmillan and Co., 1895), pp. 16, 21–22.

22 Charles Germain de Saint-Aubin, *Art of the Embroiderer* (Los Angeles: Los Angeles County Museum of Art, 1983), 44.

Glossary

aesthetic dress: Style of dress that developed as an alternative to the highly structured and confining clothing of the late nineteenth century; often characterized by natural dyes, limited boning, and a historical appearance. Individuals who favored this type of dress often traveled in intellectual circles.

Anglomania: European cultural fascination with all things English, first arising in the late eighteenth century

aniline: Chemical used by William Henry Perkin in 1856 to produce the first synthetic dyes for fabric. Such synthetic dyes were later known as aniline dyes.

appliqué: Shaped pieces of cloth stitched to the surface of a fabric background, creating a decorative element to a garment or accessory

armscye: The armhole or fabric edge to which the sleeve is sewn

art nouveau: International art movement (incorporating the visual arts, architecture, decorative arts, and fashion) that peaked around the turn of the twentieth century in reaction to the academic art styles of the nineteenth century; characterized by organic, curvilinear forms, particularly plant motifs

baleen: Hardened, hairlike fibers found in the mouths of baleen whales that filter small marine animals and plants from seawater. Used as a stiffening agent in some garments and undergarments, most notably bodices, corsets, and hoop petticoats. Also known as whalebone.

banyan: Man's dressing gown that opens down the front and was worn for informal dress; adapted by Europeans from Far Eastern and Middle Eastern garments in the seventeenth century

Belle Epoque: French for "Beautiful Era." Historical period lasting from roughly 1870 to World War I.

beret sleeves: Short puffed sleeves that are widest in the middle, reminiscent of the shape of a *béret* cap

bergère hat: Flat-brimmed straw hat with a shallow crown. *Bergère* is French for shepherdess, and this type of hat carried with it pastoral and rustic connotations, though it was a popular high-fashion accessory throughout Europe in the mid-eighteenth century.

Berlin work: Type of canvas work/needlepoint usually worked in wool yarns following a printed graphed pattern that clearly indicates the color for each stitch

bertha: Deep collarlike flounce, usually lace, encircling a wide, low neckline; popular in the mid-nineteenth century

bespoke: Term used to describe an item custom-made to the customer's individual specifications

bicorne: Two-cornered hat adopted as part of fashionable and military dress in the late eighteenth century. It was retained as part of military and court uniforms into the twentieth century.

bizarre silk: Silk textile characterized by large-scale asymmetrical patterns with both real and fantastic botanical motifs. Inspired by Asian textiles, bizarre silks were woven in France, England, and Italy in the late seventeenth and early eighteenth centuries.

bobbin lace: Lace made by braiding or twisting together threads worked upon a pillow (also known as pillow lace). The ends of the threads were wound around small spools called bobbins, which often were made of bone or ivory (bone lace).

bobbin net: Simple machine-made lace made to look like bobbin lace. Its production was made possible by John Heathcoat's bobbin-net machine, patented in 1809.

bowler hat: Hard felt hat with a rounded crown developed in England in 1849. Also known as a derby, billycock, or coke hat.

brassière: Undergarment worn to support the breasts. *Brassières* began to replace corsets in the late nineteenth century.

broderie anglaise: White-work technique in which eyelets are reinforced with embroidery stitches, usually buttonhole or overcast, and then cut out of the base fabric. England, Ireland, and Scotland were important centers of production. Popular throughout the nineteenth and early twentieth centuries.

buckskin: Leather made of buck (deer) hide

busk: Long piece of wood, whalebone, horn, or steel inserted in the center front of a corset to keep the corset rigid and the torso erect

bust bodice: Short, tight-fitting bodice worn around the bust and midriff

bustle: Understructure for thrusting the skirt back and outward from the waist

button stand: Separate band of cloth stitched along the front edge of a garment to carry buttons or buttonholes; tailoring technique first used in men's coats in the early nineteenth century

caftan: A full-length, long-sleeved garment worn as part of traditional dress in parts of the Middle East, North Africa, and Eastern Europe

cage crinoline: Petticoat understructure developed in 1856 composed of graduated steel hoops worn to give shape to the overskirt. Its antecedent, the crinoline, is a petticoat composed of a stiff horsehair-and-linen-blend fabric.

calico: See **chintz**

cane: Hollow stem of giant reeds used as a substitute for baleen

caraco: Woman's hip-length jacket worn with a petticoat for informal daywear during the eighteenth century

cashmere: Fine-quality wool derived from the underdown of Kashmir goats. From the late eighteenth century, once Kashmir garments were imported to Europe in large quantities, it became known as cashmere (English) or *cachemire* (French). By the nineteenth century, Europeans were weaving their own cashmere textiles using imported wool.

chain stitch: Embroidery that produces a row of interlocked circular stitches (resembling a "chain") on the surface of fabric

charmeuse: Soft, lightweight silk satin fabric (see **satin**)

chiffon: Lightweight, plain-weave, sheer fabric made in silk, cotton, or synthetic fibers

chiné/chiné à la branche: French term for textiles dyed according to the ikat resist-dye method (see **ikat**). *Chiné* textiles were woven in Lyon, France, from the mid-eighteenth century.

chinoiserie: Term applied to those styles of European decorative art that imitated the conventions of Chinese artistic traditions

chintz: Cotton cloth with a design painted or printed, mordant-dyed, and resist-dyed made in India, usually for export to Europe. Anglicized term for the Hindi word *chitta*, meaning "spotted cloth." Also referred to as calico.

ciselé: Velvet fabric on which the pattern is formed by contrast between cut and uncut pile loops and voided sections with no pile/pile loops. French term for "chiseled."

cloth of silver: Fabric woven with a silver supplementary weft

cockade: Rosette of ribbons attached to a garment or accessory; originally a military insignia, blue, white, and red cockades indicated support of the French Revolution

cocoon coat: Woman's coat with a barrel-shaped silhouette that is widest in the middle and tapers at the hem

cord, cording: Strands of braided or woven threads stitched between two layers of material for stiffening; used in corsets, petticoats, etc.

corset: Rigid foundation garment for the torso worn over a chemise. From the sixteenth to the nineteenth century, baleen was the most common stiffening agent, though cane was employed in examples of lesser quality. Steel was more commonly used after the first quarter of the nineteenth century.

cravat: Length of fine linen, cotton, or silk, sometimes with lace, wrapped around a man's neck and tied in the front

crepe: Fabric woven with highly twisted warps and/or wefts, yielding a crinkly finished appearance

crewel work: Type of embroidery utilizing wool yarn; popular in the seventeenth and eighteenth centuries

crinolette: Hybrid petticoat understructure that combined the bustle's upward and backward projection with the tiered steel rings of the cage crinoline

crinoline: See **cage crinoline**

cutaway coat: See **tailcoat**

cutwork: Needlework technique in which sections of cloth are cut out of a foundation fabric to form the design, with the cut edges secured with embroidery stitches and/or filled with needle lace. One example of cutwork is *broderie anglaise* (see **broderie anglaise**).

damask: Patterned textile with one set of warp and one set of weft threads in which the design is formed by a contrast of binding systems. In its classic form, it is reversible, and the contrast between pattern and ground is produced by the warp and weft faces of the same weave structure (see **warp** and **weft**).

damassé: Variation on classic damask weave structure. *Damassé* textiles are monochrome fabrics with a pattern produced by a weave structure that is unlike that of the ground. (See **damask**.)

décolleté: Having a low-cut neckline

dolman: Cloaklike outergarment with semidetached sleeves resembling both a jacket and a cape

double cloth: Woven textile containing two or more sets of warps and two or more sets of wefts that form a two-layered cloth

drawers: Bifurcated knee-length underwear made of two wide leg sections that were gathered at the waist and knees. Until approximately World War I, drawers had an opening at the middle of the inseam; thereafter, fully closed inseams were more common.

Empire silhouette: Characterized by a long, columnar gown with a high waistline inspired by the dress of ancient Greek and Roman statues. The term *Empire* refers to the period of the First French Empire (1804–14), although the style developed somewhat earlier, during the French Revolution (1789–99).

engageantes: Ruffles of lace or woven fabric (usually a lightweight cotton or linen) attached to sleeve openings near the elbow. *Engageantes* were a popular female dress accessory for most of the eighteenth century and again in the mid-nineteenth century.

eyelet: Small hole reinforced with embroidery as part of a design; alternatively, a small hole intended for lacing or fastening, often reinforced with a metal grommet, cord, or piece of leather

faille: Type of ribbed taffeta in which the weft is heavier or thicker than the warp

fanchon: Type of bonnet popular circa 1860 characterized by a short brim and a "curtain" at the nape of the neck

fichu: Square or triangular kerchief worn by women in the eighteenth and nineteenth centuries as a modesty piece to cover an exposed neck

filé: Smooth thread composed of a *lamella* wound around a core (see **lamella**)

float: Area of the warp and/or weft elements that traverse over two or more opposing elements

floss: Untwisted silk or mercerized cotton thread used for embroidery and other types of trim

flounce: Decorative length of textile or lace applied to a garment

fly fringe: Fringe or cord with attached knots and bunches of floss; used to decorate garments and accessories (see **floss**)

French knots: Embroidery yarns coiled and looped above the surface fabric to form slightly raised knots

frisé: Crinkled thread composed of two plied-silk threads or silk thread and *lamella* in which one component is twisted more tightly than the other to produce a spiral effect (see **lamella**)

frock: Archaic English term for a long, loose gown or undergarment worn by both men and women. Over time, the term was increasingly used to refer to women's dresses but was retained in menswear for the loose, full-skirted frock coat; also a young boy's gown worn until the age of five or six, when he was old enough to wear breeches.

frock coat: Man's coat style that became fashionable in the eighteenth century; nineteenth-century styles were characterized by full skirts and turned-down collars

full finish: Process in which woolen textiles undergo shrinking and combing, resulting in a tight weave and a soft, fluffy nap

gaufrure: French embroidery term used to describe a technique in which threads are interlaced to create a wafflelike or basket-weave effect

gauze: Weave structure in which paired warps cross one another in a series of figure eights with weft elements passing through them at regular intervals, resulting in an open-mesh fabric

gilt: Gilded, or coated, with a fine layer of gold

gore: Triangular piece of fabric sewn into a garment to increase width; sometimes called a gusset

guipure: French embroidery term used to describe a technique in which threads are stitched over a piece of vellum or parchment in order to give the embroidery a raised effect

haute couture: French term that literally means "high sewing"; haute couture garments are made to order for a specific customer to her dimensions and usually incorporate fine fabrics and hand-sewing techniques.

hoop petticoat: Underpetticoat stiffened with cane or baleen hoops; worn circa 1710–1820

ikat: Resist-dyeing process that is part of long-standing Asian textile traditions. In the ikat method, prior to weaving, bundles of warp or weft (and sometimes both) elements are tied and then submerged into a dye bath. A pattern then emerges on the threads in which the tied segments remain free of dye and the untied sections absorb color. Once the threads are woven into a textile, the dyed and undyed sections produce an all-over pattern with a blurry effect. (See **resist-dyeing**.)

incroyable: Man wearing the exaggerated, highly stylized dress of the Directory period (France, 1795–99); from the French word for incredible

indigo: Dye plant that produces blue- and green-colored dyes. The coloring principle is contained in the leaves and manifested through oxidation. Indigo is ideally suited for resist-dyeing (see **resist-dyeing**).

Jacquard loom: Mechanized loom, invented in France in 1801 by Joseph-Marie Charles Jacquard, that allowed manufacturers to produce textiles with complex patterns and weave structures at a faster rate and lower cost relative to comparable hand-loomed textiles. The Jacquard loom involved an innovative use of punch cards that contained the program for the textile pattern. Jacquard's punch card system is regarded as an important technological forerunner of the modern computer.

lamella: Flat strip of metal, or gilt or silvered leather, membrane, or paper used for yarn in weaving or embroidery

lampas: Complex textile weave with more than one set of warp and weft elements. This type of cloth was woven in Europe from the tenth century and was difficult and costly to produce. (See **warp** and **weft**.)

lappets: Woman's headdress component worn from the late seventeenth to the nineteenth century; long streamers of lace or a white textile worn attached to a cap or applied directly to hair

leg-of-mutton: Sleeve style resembling the shape of a leg of mutton; popular in the 1830s and again in the 1890s. Also known as *gigot* (French for "leg of lamb") sleeves.

Liberty & Co.: London department store established in 1875, which, from its beginnings, featured luxury items imported from the Far East, earning it the nickname, "Eastern Bazaar." In 1884, to rival Parisian fashion houses, the company started its own clothing line; many of its in-house designers were influenced by the arts and crafts and art nouveau movements.

lounge jacket: Short coat or jacket with a straight back and no seam at the waist. Also known as a sack coat.

Marseilles embroidery: White-work technique popular in the eighteenth century featuring corded quilting and embroidery. Important centers of production included southern France and Italy. (See **white-work**.)

mignonettes: Small-scale geometric or floral patterns found on printed cotton textiles

miser purse: Small tubular purse, usually knitted, used by both men and women throughout much of the nineteenth century. A small opening in the midsection of the purse, through which the carrier could insert coins or other small objects, was secured by two sliding rings.

mitts: Fingerless "gloves" that reach the elbow; popular in the eighteenth century. Knitted, wrist-length versions were popular in the nineteenth century.

M-notch: M-shaped notch used in men's suits to facilitate a smooth transition between the turned-down collar and the lapel. Common from 1803 until roughly 1850; thereafter employed in men's formal wear until about 1870.

moiré: Textile finishing process in which a ribbed fabric is pressed with metal rollers so that some of the ribs are flattened while others are not and therefore reflect light differently. The resulting effect is a rippled or wavelike sheen. Silks treated this way are sometimes referred to as "watered" silks.

monobosom: In the late nineteenth and early twentieth centuries, with the advent of the S-curve corset, the unified shape of the bust was called monobosom.

mordant: Substance applied to cloth before dyeing to ensure that dyes bond permanently to the cloth

morning coat: Single-breasted coat that shares characteristics with the tailcoat and frock coat. Distinguished by a gradually curved hem that slopes down from the center front and extends into broad tails at the back. The style emerged in the mid-nineteenth century, but by the last decades of the century was increasingly reserved for formal wear. Morning coats are still worn for formal daywear today.

muslin: Fine, sheer, plain-weave cotton first imported from India, then produced in Europe, particularly England and France

needle lace: Lace worked with needle and thread consisting primarily of buttonhole stitches worked over an outlining thread attached to a paper pattern

open work: Decorative needlework (such as drawn or pulled threadwork and cutwork) that results in a pattern of small holes in a foundation fabric

pagoda sleeves: Funnel-shaped sleeves that are widest at the hem; named for the Asian tiered tower

paletot: Unfitted jacket or short overcoat; originally a man's garment, it became part of the feminine wardrobe in the nineteenth century.

panier: Wide hoop petticoat stiffened with cane or baleen; worn in the eighteenth century to extend women's skirts out on both sides. French term for "basket." (See **cane** and **baleen**.)

paning: Technique in which long openings are inserted into a garment through which a lining or undergarment can be seen; popular during the Renaissance and revived in the late eighteenth and early nineteenth centuries

pantalettes: Undergarments that covered the legs and extended just below the knee. Worn by women during the early nineteenth century until approximately 1830, and by girls and very young boys until the mid-nineteenth century. Sometimes referred to as pantaloons or trousers, particularly with respect to children's clothing.

pantaloons: Man's tight, fitted trousers that extend to the ankle; supplanted knee breeches in the late eighteenth and early nineteenth centuries

passementerie: Elaborate trimmings, such as applied braid, cord, fringe, lace, or beadwork

paste: Glass cut and polished to look like gems

peplum: Short, gathered, pleated, and/or trimmed piece of fabric attached at the waist of a woman's dress or jacket to create a flared or draped effect

petit point: Needlepoint done on a canvas ground; from the French for "little point"

petticoat: During the eighteenth century, the term *petticoat* was used to refer to a skirt or to the underskirt that provided shape and support to a skirt or gown (such as a hoop petticoat; see **hoop petticoat**). From around the mid-nineteenth century, the term generally referred to an underskirt or half-slip.

pile: Supplementary threads that are raised above the ground fabric, giving a three-dimensional effect

pin-tuck: Very narrow tuck; a fold or pleat that is sewn in place on a piece of fabric

piqué: Fine-ribbed fabric, usually made of cotton

plain weave: This basic weave structure consists of a weft element that passes over one warp element, then under one warp element, and so on. Also called tabby weave. (See **warp** and **weft**.)

princess line: Construction technique for a fitted garment cut without a seam at the waist and shaped by vertical seams that extend from neck to hem

purl: Tightly coiled fine metal wire used in embroidery

ramoneur: *Ramoneur* fabrics were printed cottons with dark background colors, such as black and brown. This French term means "chimney sweep."

redingote: Man's overcoat with overlapping front skirts and wide collar; also a woman's similar coatlike outergarment or dress with long sleeves and a full-length open skirt. The name is the French corruption of the English "riding coat."

resist-dyeing: Techniques in which designs are applied to a cloth with paste or wax or by tie-dyed methods; the dye then permeates only those parts of the cloth that are left free from the resist material.

reticule: Small pouch bag, often with a drawstring top

revers: Also known as lapel; the turned-back edge of a coat, vest, or bodice

robe à l'anglaise: "English dress" characterized by a close-fitting bodice

robe à la française: "French dress" characterized by a draped back with double box pleats that hang loose from the shoulders to the ground

robe à la polonaise: "Polish dress" characterized by the draped skirt of an ankle-length robe or gown that reveals a petticoat or underskirt; often worn for walking

rouleau: Tube of fabric; often filled with wadding to give it a firm shape. *Rouleaux* often were attached to the bottom of skirts to decorate, stiffen, and add weight to the hem.

ruched: Loosely pleated, shirred, or gathered

ruff: Neckwear worn by men and women in the sixteenth and seventeenth centuries characterized by radiating starched and stiffened pleats of linen or lace attached to a neckband; often consisting of multiple layers of fabric. Revived in the early nineteenth century.

sampler: Length of cloth on which needlework motifs or techniques are practiced, stored for reference, or demonstrated as proof of skill

sans-culottes: French term meaning "without breeches." The phrase emerged during the French Revolution to describe the poorer Revolutionaries who wore working-class trousers as opposed to the breeches (in French, *culottes*) worn by the elite.

satin: Weaving technique characterized by warp elements that pass over multiple weft elements (warp floats), or vice versa (weft floats). These long floats are what give satin fabric its characteristic sheen. (See **warp** and **weft**.)

satin stitch: Technique in which successive embroidery stitches are worked side by side, with the needle returning on the back side of the embroidery to the starting point of the last stitch

selvage: The self-finished edges of a fabric. The warpwise edge of a textile in which wefts encircle the outer warp elements.

sequin: Flat disk applied to fabric for decoration typically made of metal, with a hole in the middle

shot silk: Silk fabric consisting of warp and weft elements of two or more different colors, resulting in an iridescent appearance. Also known as changeable silk.

sleeve plumpers: Accessory "pillows" worn underneath women's short, full sleeves to provide support and fullness; popular in the 1820s and 1830s

smocking: Embroidery technique in which fabric is gathered and made expandable; used particularly on cuffs, bodices, and necklines before the development of elastic

spencer: Above-the-waist, close-fitting jacket worn for a short time by men but quickly adopted by women and children in the early nineteenth century

stays: See **corset**

steam-molding: Process invented in 1868 by Edwin Izod in which the corset is placed on heated metal forms, starched, and steamed into shape. A corset treated in this manner was extremely rigid and capable of fashioning a body into a standard, idealized shape.

stock: Man's neck cloth tied or fastened around the neck without any loose, hanging ends

stomacher: V-shaped, usually decorative panel worn by women in the seventeenth and eighteenth centuries to fill in the front of the bodice between the edges of an open gown

supplementary warp or weft: Secondary set of warp or weft elements used to create pattern in the woven design of a textile (see **warp** and **weft**)

taffeta: Light, crisp, plain-woven fabric made of fine silk (see **plain weave**)

tailcoat: Coat with the front of the skirt cut away in a straight line at the waist, leaving only the rear section of the skirt, known as the tails. Also known as a cutaway coat.

tambour: Type of embroidery worked in chain stitch with a hooked needle on fabric stretched onto a circular frame. Cloth stretched tight in this manner looked like a drum, hence the name *tambour*, which is French for "drum."

tapestry weave: Weft-faced plain weave, usually with a discontinuous weft. More complex varieties of tapestry weave include double-interlocking and interlocking-twill-tapestry weave.

tartan: Plaid woolen twill cloth traditionally worn in the Scottish Highlands

tea gown: Loose gown worn at home for afternoon entertaining. A European innovation that appropriated the flowing lines and luxurious fabrics of traditional Asian garments. These gowns became popular as a relaxed alternative to the rigid corsets and tightly fitted garments of the late nineteenth century.

top boots: Boots worn for hunting in the eighteenth century, later adopted for fashionable dress; characterized by black leather bottoms and tan leather tops

top hat: Tall, flat-crowned, broad-brimmed hat. A popular accessory in menswear from the late eighteenth through the early twentieth century.

tremblant: Jewelry ornament with segments that tremble when the object is subjected to movement. From the French word for "trembling."

tricorne: Three-cornered hat popular in the late seventeenth and eighteenth centuries

tulle: Lightweight, fine netting; often starched

tunic: Long-sleeved, T-shaped garment

turban: Headdress consisting of materials folded and stitched to simulate the Asian and Middle Eastern headdress of the same name

twill: Weave structure in which one set of warp and weft elements passes over two or more elements and under one or more elements of the opposing set to form floats in a diagonal alignment, which produces a characteristic "stepped" appearance. Some examples of twill-woven fabrics are chino, denim, gabardine, and tweed. (See **warp** and **weft**.)

twist: Twisted and plied embroidery/sewing thread

velvet: Textile with cut or uncut pile woven on either a plain weave, twill, or satin foundation. During the weaving process, metal rods are inserted in order to raise the warp into loops. Secured in place with wefts, the rods can then be removed to reveal a looped pile, or, prior to the removal of the rods, the raised warps can be sliced to create a cut pile (see **pile**, **warp**, and **weft**).

vest: See **waistcoat**

waistcoat: Man's garment worn under the coat as part of the three-piece suit. It grew shorter throughout the eighteenth century, and by about 1780, it was waist-length and more often referred to as a vest.

warp: In weaving, warp elements are the lengthwise (or vertical) threads through which the weft elements are woven. When weaving on a loom, the warp elements are attached to the loom frame at both ends before weaving of the weft threads begins.

weft: In weaving, weft (also called woof) elements are those that pass crosswise over and under the warp elements to create a fabric.

whalebone: See **baleen**

white-work: General term for a range of embroidery techniques involving a white ground fabric and white embroidery yarns

Selected Bibliography

Adburgham, Alison. *Liberty's: A Biography of a Shop.* London: George Allen & Unwin, 1975.

Albrecht-Mathey, Elisabeth. *The Fabrics of Mulhouse and Alsace 1750–1800.* Leigh-on-Sea, England: F. Lewis Publishers, 1968.

Ames, Frank. *The Kashmir Shawl and Its Indo-French Influence.* England: Antique Collectors' Club, 1986.

Arch, Nigel, and Joanna Marschner. *Splendour at Court: Dressing for Royal Occasions since 1700.* London and Sydney: Unwin Hyman, 1987.

Arizzoli-Clémentel, Pierre, and Pascale Gorguet Ballesteros. *Fastes de cour et cérémonies royales: Le costume de cour en Europe 1650–1800*, exh. cat. Paris: Réunion des musées nationaux, 2009.

Arnold, Janet. *Patterns of Fashion: Englishwomen's Dresses & Their Construction c. 1660–1860.* London: Wace and Company, 1964.

Arnold, Janet. *Patterns of Fashion: Englishwomen's Dresses & Their Construction c. 1860–1940.* London: Wace and Company, 1966.

Ashelford, Jane. *The Art of Dress: Clothes and Society, 1500–1914.* London: National Trust Enterprises, 1996.

Barnes, Ruth, Steven Cohen, and Rosemary Crill. *Trade, Temple & Court: Indian Textiles from the Tapi Collection.* Mumbai: India Book House, 2002.

Beck, Thomasina. *The Embroiderer's Garden.* England: David & Charles Publishers, 1988.

Beer, Alice Baldwin. *Trade Goods: A Study of Indian Chintz in the Collection of the Cooper-Hewitt Museum of Decorative Arts and Design, Smithsonian Institution.* Washington, D.C.: Smithsonian Institution Press, 1970.

Berenson, Kathryn. *Quilts of Provence: The Art and Craft of French Quiltmaking.* New York: Henry Holt and Company, 1996.

Binder, Pearl. *The Peacock's Tail.* London: George Harrap & Co., 1958.

Blum, Stella, ed. *Eighteenth-Century French Fashions in Full Color: 64 Engravings from the "Galerie des Modes," 1778–1787.* New York: Dover Publications, 1982.

Browne, Clare. *Lace: From the Victoria and Albert Museum.* New York: Harry N. Abrams, 2004.

Buck, Anne. *Clothes and the Child: A Handbook of Children's Dress in England 1500–1900.* New York: Holmes & Meier, 1996.

Buck, Anne. *Dress in Eighteenth-Century England.* New York: Holmes & Meier, 1979.

Buck, Anne. *Victorian Costume and Costume Accessories.* London: Herbert Jenkins, 1961.

Byrde, Penelope. *Jane Austen Fashion: Fashion and Needlework in the Works of Jane Austen.* Ludlow, Shropshire: Excellent Press, 1999.

Byrde, Penelope. *The Male Image: Men's Fashion in Britain 1300–1970.* London: B. T. Batsford, 1979.

Byrde, Penelope. *Nineteenth Century Fashion.* London: B. T. Batsford, 1992.

Carter, Alison. *Underwear: The Fashion History.* New York: Drama Book Publishers, 1992.

Chapman, S. D., and S. Chassagne. *European Textile Printers in the Eighteenth Century: A Study of Peel and Oberkampf.* London: Heinemann Educational Books, 1981.

Coleman, Elizabeth Ann. *The Opulent Era: Fashions of Worth, Doucet and Pingat.* London: Thames & Hudson and the Brooklyn Museum, 1989.

Crill, Rosemary. *Chintz: Indian Textiles for the West.* London: V&A Publications, 2008.

Crill, Rosemary. *Indian Embroidery.* London: V&A Publications, 1999.

Crill, Rosemary, Jennifer Wearden, and Verity Wilson. *Dress in Detail from around the World.* London: V&A Publications, 2002.

Cumming, Valerie. *Royal Dress: The Image and the Reality 1580 to the Present Day.* New York: Holmes & Meier, 1989.

Cumming, Valerie. *The Visual History of Costume Accessories.* New York: Costume & Fashion Press, 1998.

Cunningham, Patricia A. *Reforming Women's Fashion, 1850–1920: Politics, Health, and Art.* Kent, OH, and London: The Kent State University Press, 2003.

Cunnington, C. Willett and Phillis, with revisions by A. D. Mansfield and Valerie Mansfield. *The History of Underclothes.* London: Faber & Faber, 1981.

Cunnington, Phillis, and Alan Mansfield. *English Costume for Sports and Outdoor Recreation from the Sixteenth to the Nineteenth Centuries.* London: Adam and Charles Black, 1969.

Davis, Mildred J. *The Art of Crewel Embroidery.* New York: Crown Publishers, 1962.

De Marly, Diana. *Fashion for Men: An Illustrated History.* New York: Holmes & Meier, 1985.

De Marly, Diana. *Worth: Father of Haute Couture.* New York: Holmes & Meier, 1990.

Delpierre, Madeleine. *Dress in France in the Eighteenth Century.* New Haven, CT, and London: Yale University Press, 1997.

Delpierre, Madeleine, et al. *Modes & revolutions, 1780–1804*, exh. cat. Paris: Éditions Paris-Musées, 1989.

Earnshaw, Pat. *How to Recognise Machine Laces.* Guildford, England: Gorse Publications, 1995.

Earnshaw, Pat. *Lace in Fashion: From the Sixteenth to the Twentieth Centuries.* London: B. T. Batsford, 1985.

Earnshaw, Pat. *Lace Machines and Machine Laces.* London: B. T. Batsford, 1986.

Ewing, Elizabeth. *Dress and Undress: A History of Women's Underwear.* New York: Drama Book Specialists, 1978.

Ewing, Elizabeth. *Underwear: A History.* New York: Theatre Arts Books, 1972.

Falkenberg, Regine, Adelheid Rasche, and Christine Waidenschalger, eds. *On Men: Masculine Dress Code from the Ancient Greeks to Cowboys.* Berlin: International Committee for Museums and Collections of Costume, 2005.

Farrell-Beck, Jane. "Nineteenth-Century Construction Techniques: Practice and Purpose." *Dress*, Vol. 13, 1987: 11–20.

Fields, Jill. *An Intimate Affair: Women, Lingerie, and Sexuality.* Berkeley: University of California Press, 2007.

Fortune, Brandon Brame. "Studious Men Are Always Painted in Gowns: Charles Willson Peale's *Benjamin Rush* and the Question of Banyans in Eighteenth-Century Anglo-American Portraiture." *Dress*, Vol. 29, 2002: 27–40.

Foster, Vanda. *Bags and Purses.* London: B. T. Batsford, 1982.

Foster, Vanda. *A Visual History of Costume: The Nineteenth Century.* London: B. T. Batsford, 1986.

Fukai, Akiko, et al. *Fashion: The Collection of the Kyoto Costume Institute: A History from the 18th to the 20th Century.* Köln, Germany, and Los Angeles: Taschen, 2002.

Gillow, John, and Nicholas Barnard. *Traditional Indian Textiles.* London: Thames & Hudson, 1991.

Grimble, Frances. *Fashions of the Gilded Age*, Vols. 1 and 2. San Francisco: Lavolta Press, 2004.

Gruber, Alain. *Ancien Régime–Premier Empire, 1785–1805: L'Art textile et la toilette*, exh. cat. Riggisberg, Switzerland: Abegg-Stiftung, 1989.

Gwynne, Judyth L. *The Illustrated Dictionary of Lace.* London: B. T. Batsford, 1997.

Haertig, Evelyn. *More Beautiful Purses.* Carmel, CA: Gallery Graphics Press, 1990.

Hart, Avril, and Susan North. *Historical Fashion in Detail: The 17th and 18th Centuries.* London: V&A Publications, 1998.

Hartkamp-Jonxis, Ebeltje. *Sitsen uit India: Indian Chintzes.* Amsterdam: Rijksmuseum Amsterdam, 1994.

Holden, Angus. *Elegant Modes in the Nineteenth Century: From High Waist to Bustle.* London: George Allen & Unwin, 1935.

Irwin, John, and Katharine B. Brett. *Origins of Chintz.* London: Her Majesty's Stationery Office, 1970.

Irwin, John, and Margaret Hall. *Indian Embroideries*, Vol. 2 in series *Historic Textiles of India at the Calico Museum.* Ahmedabad, India: S. R. Bastikar on behalf of Calico Museum of Textiles, 1973.

Johansen, Katia. *Royal Gowns*, exh. cat. Copenhagen: Rosenborg Palace, 1990.

Johnson, Judy M. *French Fashion Plates of the Romantic Era in Full Color: 120 Plates from the "Petit Courrier des Dames," 1830–34.* New York: Dover Publications, 1991.

Johnston, Lucy, with Marion Kite and Helen Persson. *Nineteenth-Century Fashion in Detail.* London: V&A Publications, 2005.

Johnstone, Pauline. *Three Hundred Years of Embroidery: 1600–1900: Treasures from the Collection of the Embroiderers' Guild of Great Britain.* Adelaide: Wakefield Press, 1986.

Koda, Harold, and Andrew Bolton. *Dangerous Liaisons: Fashion and Furniture in the Eighteenth Century*, exh. cat. New York: The Metropolitan Museum of Art; New Haven, CT, and London: Yale University Press, 2006.

Kuchta, David. *The Three-Piece Suit and Modern Masculinity: England, 1550–1850.* Berkeley: University of California Press, 2002.

Kuchta, David M. " 'Graceful, Virile, and Useful': The Origins of the Three-piece Suit." *Dress*, Vol. 17, 1990: 118–126.

The Kyoto Costume Institute. *Mōdo no jyaponisumu (Japonism in Fashion)*, exh. cat. Kyoto: The Kyoto Costume Institute, 1996.

The Kyoto Costume Institute. *Shintai no yume: Fasshon or mienai korusetto (Visions of the Body: Fashion or Invisible Corset)*, exh. cat. Kyoto: The Kyoto Costume Institute, 1999.

Lansdell, Avril. *Seaside Fashions 1860–1939.* Princes Risborough, Buckinghamshire: Shire Publications, 1990.

Le Bourhis, Katell, ed. *The Age of Napoleon: Costume from Revolution to Empire, 1789–1815*, exh. cat. New York: The Metropolitan Museum of Art and Harry N. Abrams, 1989.

Lee-Whitman, Leanna. "The Silk Trade: Chinese Silks and the British East India Company." *Winterthur Portfolio*, Vol. 17, No. 1, Spring 1982: 21–41.

Levey, Santina M. *Lace: A History.* London: Victoria & Albert Museum and W. S. Maney & Son, 1983.

Lévi-Strauss, Monique. *The Cashmere Shawl.* London: Dryad Press, 1987.

Maeder, Edward, et al. *An Elegant Art: Fashion & Fantasy in the Eighteenth Century*, exh. cat. Los Angeles: Los Angeles County Museum of Art; New York: Harry N. Abrams, 1983.

Mansel, Philip. *Dressed to Rule: Royal and Court Costume from Louis XIV to Elizabeth II.* New Haven, CT, and London: Yale University Press, 2005.

Mansfield, Alan. *Ceremonial Costume: Court, Civil and Civic Costume from 1660 to the Present Day.* Totowa, NJ: Barnes & Noble Books, 1980.

Marsh, Gail. *18th Century Embroidery Techniques.* Lewes, East Sussex: Guild of Master Craftsman Publications, 2006.

Marsh, Gail. *19th Century Embroidery Techniques.* Lewes, East Sussex: Guild of Master Craftsman Publications, 2008.

Martin, Richard. *The Ceaseless Century: 300 Years of Eighteenth-Century Costume*, exh. cat. New York: The Metropolitan Museum of Art, 2000.

Martin, Richard, and Harold Koda. *Infra-Apparel*, exh. cat. New York: The Metropolitan Museum of Art, 1993.

Martin, Richard, and Harold Koda. *Orientalism: Visions of the East in Western Dress*, exh. cat. New York: The Metropolitan Museum of Art and Harry N. Abrams, 1994.

Meij, Ietse. *Haute couture & prêt-à-porter: Mode 1750–2000: A Choice from the Costume Collection, Municipal Museum, The Hague.* The Hague: Gemeentemuseum; Zwolle: Waanders, 1998.

Montgomery, Florence M. *Printed Textiles: English and American Cottons and Linens 1700–1850.* New York: Viking Press, 1970.

Morra, Marisa. "Silent Informers: Men's Coats from a 19th Century Period of Transition." *Dress*, Vol. 11, 1985: 68–76.

Morrell, Anne. *The Techniques of Indian Embroidery.* Loveland, CO: Interweave Press, 1995.

Murray, Anne. "From Breeches to Sherryvallies." *Waffen- und Kostumkunde*, Vol. 16, No. 2, 1974; reprinted in *Dress*, Vol. 2, No. 1, 1976: 17–33.

Musée de la mode et du costume. *Au paradis des dames: Nouveautés, modes et confections 1810–1870*, exh. cat. Paris: Éditions Paris-Musées, 1992.

Musée des Arts et Traditions populaires de moyenne Provence. *Le costume populaire provençal.* Aix-en-Provence: Edisud, *1990.*

Musée Galliera. *Le Coton et la Mode: 1000 ans d'aventures*, exh. cat. Paris: Éditions Paris-Musées, 2000.

Musée Galliera. *Modes en miroir: La France et la Hollande au temps des Lumières*, exh. cat. Paris: Éditions Paris-Musées, 2005.

Musée Galliera. *Sous l'Empire des crinolines*, exh. cat. Paris: Éditions Paris-Musées, 2008.

Museo del Tessuto Prato. *Five Centuries of Italian Textiles: 1300–1800*, exh. cat. Prato, Italy: Museo del Tessuto, 1981.

Nemati, Parviz. *Shawls of the East: From Kerman to Kashmir.* New York: PDN Publishing, 2003.

Newton, Stella Mary. *Health, Art & Reason: Dress Reformers of the 19th Century.* London: John Murray, 1974.

Parker, Rozsika. *The Subversive Stitch: Embroidery and the Making of the Feminine.* New York: Routledge, 1989.

Pellegrin, Nicole. *Les vêtements de la liberté.* Aix-en-Provence: Éditions Alinea, 1989.

Perrot, Philippe. *Fashioning the Bourgeoisie: A History of Clothing in the Nineteenth Century.* Princeton, NJ: Princeton University Press, 1994.

Purdy, Daniel L., ed. *The Rise of Fashion: A Reader.* Minneapolis and London: University of Minnesota Press, 2004.

Ribeiro, Aileen. *The Art of Dress: Fashion in England and France 1750 to 1820.* New Haven, CT, and London: Yale University Press, 1995.

Ribeiro, Aileen. *Dress in Eighteenth-Century Europe 1715–1789.* New Haven, CT, and London: Yale University Press, 2002.

Ribeiro, Aileen. *Fashion in the French Revolution.* London: B. T. Batsford, 1988.

Ribeiro, Aileen. *A Visual History of Costume: The Eighteenth Century.* London: B. T. Batsford, 1983.

Ribeiro, Aileen, and Valerie Cumming. *The Visual History of Costume.* New York: Drama Book Publishers, 1989.

Riffel, Mélanie, and Sophie Rouart. *Toile de Jouy: Printed Textiles in the Classic French Style.* London: Thames & Hudson, 2003.

Saint-Aubin, Charles Germain de. *Art of the Embroiderer.* Los Angeles: Los Angeles County Museum of Art, 1983.

Schoeser, Mary. "A Secret Trade: Plate-Printed Textiles and Dress Accessories, ca. 1620–1820." *Dress*, Vol. 34, 2007: 49–59.

Schoeser, Mary. *Silk.* New Haven, CT, and London: Yale University Press, 2007.

Schoeser, Mary, and Kathleen Dejardin. *French Textiles: From 1760 to the Present.* London: Laurence King, 1991.

Serena, Raffaella. *Berlin Work: Samplers and Embroidery of the Nineteenth Century.* South Kearny, NJ: DMC; Berkeley, CA: LACIS, 1996.

Simon, Marie. *Fashion in Art: The Second Empire and Impressionism.* London: Zwemmer, 1995.

Sonday, Milton. "Damask: Definition and Technique." In Schorta, Regula, ed., *Leinendamaste: Produktionszentren und Sammlungen.* Riggisberger Berichte, Vol. 7. Riggisberg, Switzerland: Abegg-Stiftung, 1999: 113–130.

Staniland, Kay. *In Royal Fashion: The Clothes of Princess Charlotte of Wales & Queen Victoria 1796–1901*, exh. cat. London: Museum of London, 1997.

Starobinski, Jean, et al. *Revolution in Fashion: European Clothing, 1715–1815*, exh. cat. New York: Abbeville Press, 1989.

Steele, Valerie. *The Corset: A Cultural History.* New Haven, CT, and London: Yale University Press, 2001.

Steele, Valerie. *Paris Fashion: A Cultural History.* New York: Oxford University Press, 1988.

Styles, John. *The Dress of the People: Everyday Fashion in Eighteenth-Century England.* New Haven, CT, and London: Yale University Press, 2007.

Swain, Margaret. *Figures on Fabric: Embroidery Design Sources and Their Application.* London: Adam and Charles Black, 1980.

Synge, Lanto. *Art of Embroidery: History of Style and Technique.* England: Antique Collectors' Club, 2001.

Tarrant, Naomi. *The Development of Costume.* New York: Routledge, 1994.

Thompson, Angela. *Embroidery with Beads.* London: B. T. Batsford, 1987.

Thornton, Peter. *Baroque and Rococo Silks.* New York: Taplinger Publishing Co., 1965.

Troy, Nancy J. *Couture Culture: A Study in Modern Art and Fashion.* Cambridge, MA: The MIT Press, 2003.

Tuchscherer, Jean-Michel. *The Fabrics of Mulhouse and Alsace, 1801–1850.* Leigh-on-Sea, England: F. Lewis Publishers, 1972.

Vrignaud, Gilberte. *Vêture et parure en France au dix-huitième siècle.* Paris: Éditions Messene, 1995.

Wardle, Patricia. *Victorian Lace.* New York: Frederick A. Praeger Publishers, 1969.

Waugh, Norah. *Corsets and Crinolines.* New York: Theatre Arts Books, 1970.

Waugh, Norah. *The Cut of Men's Clothes, 1600–1900.* New York: Theatre Arts Books, 1964.

Waugh, Norah. *The Cut of Women's Clothes, 1600–1930.* New York: Theatre Arts Books, 1968.

Whitechapel Art Gallery. *Woven Air: The Muslin & Kantha Tradition of Bangladesh*, exh. cat. London: Whitechapel Art Gallery, 1988.

Wilcox, Claire. *Bags.* London: V&A Publications, 1999.

Wilson, Erica. *Crewel Embroidery.* New York: Charles Scribner's Sons, 1962.

Wingfield Digby, George. *Elizabethan Embroidery.* London: Faber and Faber, 1963.

Wrigley, Richard. *The Politics of Appearances: Representations of Dress in Revolutionary France.* Oxford and New York: Berg, 2002.

Acknowledgments

The exciting revelations of our new historic-costume collection resulted from the concerted efforts and commitment of many people. We are extremely grateful to Michael Govan, LACMA CEO and Wallis Annenberg Director, who immediately grasped the significance of this collection and its place in the scope of the museum's holdings; his enthusiasm and promotion were essential to its acquisition. Our thanks also extend to Deputy Director Nancy Thomas, whose advocacy is valued and encouraging. Our most sincere gratitude goes to our donors—Suzanne A. Saperstein and Michael and Ellen Michelson, the Costume Council, the Edgerton Foundation, Gail and Gerald Oppenheimer, Maureen H. Shapiro, Grace Tsao, and Lenore and Richard Wayne—without whose generosity the extraordinary collection would never have been acquired.

We are deeply indebted to Nola Butler, Head of Publications, and Thomas Frick, Editor in Chief, for their remarkable efforts and tenacity in undertaking this project, and to Editor Margery L. Schwartz for her guidance and insightful edification of the book's text. The bold and powerful pageant of historic costume was sensitively and beautifully designed by Abbott Miller of Pentagram. We were delighted to collaborate with publisher Mary DelMonico of DelMonico Books-Prestel in realizing this document of LACMA's costume and textile treasures. Sharing the collection with John Galliano was an honor; we are privileged to have the book begin with his elegant and inspirational preface.

We owe a great deal of gratitude to LACMA's Photographic Services, especially to Senior Photographer Steven Oliver, whose inspired presentation of the sculptural qualities of costume and the unique character of material and technique confirms the splendor and significance of the art of dress. Senior Photographer, Conservation, Yosi Pozeilov's exacting photography was necessary for conservation documentation, and for the overwhelming task of coordinating hundreds of images, securing rights, and coordinating with the publisher, we thank Supervising Photographer Peter Brenner and Rights and Reproductions Manager Cheryle T. Robertson.

The members and associates of the Costume and Textiles Department deserve our wholehearted thanks. Administrative Assistant Nancy Lawson Carcione, with her customary resourcefulness, adeptly helped keep the project smoothly on track. Exquisitely dressed mannequins, with their imaginative period paper wigs, and the superbly crafted invisible mounts were realized by Curatorial Assistant Clarissa M. Esguerra, Collections Administrator Fionn Zarubica Lemon, and Installation Assistants Sofia Y. Gan and Melinda Webber Kerstein. We are indebted to our joint authors of the catalogue—Wallis Annenberg Curatorial Fellow Nicole LaBouff, Clarissa M. Esguerra, and Research Scholar Kimberly Chrisman-Campbell—whose ideas, invaluable counsel, and insight were critical to the concept and execution of both the exhibition and its accompanying book.

The project was enlivened by the commitment of many talented and spirited interns, who reproduced historically accurate props and undergarments and assisted with costume research. Kate Michelson, Audrey Wayne, Caitlin Talmage, Erica Scott, Claudia Gomez, Masaco Kuroda, Nicole Saint, Ashley Cohen, Melissa Castillo, Fatima Manalili, Alyson Bender, Kate Reilly, Giselle Berzenye, Lydia McHam, and Claire Vinson merit recognition and profound gratitude.

The acquisition of this collection and presentation of selected parts on display and in print resulted from the coordinated efforts of many colleagues. For the complex negotiations of acquisition, we relied on the expertise of Vice President and General Counsel Fred Goldstein and the unwavering support of Chief Financial Officer Ann Rowland and Budget and Investment Officer Mark Mitchell. We thank Terry Morello, Vice President of Development, as well as the department's Melissa Bomes, Associate Vice President, Chelsea Hadley, Director of Major Gifts, Diana Veach, Associate Vice President, Development Operations and Gift Planning, Daniel Thomas, Director of Major Donor Events, and the Development staff for steadfast assistance that was both generous and generative. The prodigious duty of accessioning such a large collection was handled with alacrity and unfailing good cheer by Associate Registrar Jennifer Yates and Assistant Registrar Angela Chen, under the direction of Head Registrar Nancy Russell. Associate Registrar Tiffany Shea and Assistant Registrar Sarah Nichols adroitly coordinated information and tracked the objects during the exhibition's installation.

The many aspects of staging an exhibition of historic costume were deftly accomplished with prowess and diplomacy by Exhibition Programs. Assistant Director Irene Martín, Senior Exhibition Programs Coordinator Sarah Minnaert, Exhibition Coordinator for Permanent Collections Nancy Meyer, and Financial Analyst Marciana Broiles are to be admired for their constant and reliable support throughout the process. We extend our appreciation for the visionary concept and dramatic design of the installation to Pier Luigi Pizzi and Massimo Pizzi Gasparon, and heartily thank LACMA's Director of Special Art Installations John Bowsher and Senior Exhibition Designer Victoria Turkel Behner and Exhibition Designer Eileen Dikdan for their capable and enthusiastic collaboration. Associate Director, Head of Graphic Design Amy McFarland, along with Graphic Designer Meghan Moran and Production Manager Karen Knapp, provided us with lively and sophisticated artwork. We owe a debt of gratitude to Barbara Pflaumer, Vice President, Communications, Allison Agsten, Director of Communications, Annie Carone, Junior Communications Associate, and other museum staff members for showing the exhibition at its best to the public.

Our ongoing appreciation is extended—as it is for all exhibitions of costume and textiles—to the members of Conservation, led by Suzanne D. Booth and David G. Booth Conservation Center Director Mark Gilberg. Senior Conservator and Head, Textiles, Catherine C. McLean, and Associate Conservator, Textiles, Susan Renate Schmalz devoted their extensive expertise and passion to the complex challenge of preparing eighteenth- and nineteenth-century dress for exhibition. They were most ably assisted by Mellon Fellow Maria Fusco, Camilla Chandler Frost Summer Intern Laleña Vellanoweth, and enthusiastic volunteer Lynn Bathke. We were continually impressed with the solutions to problematic costume mounts devised by Staff Technician Jean Neeman, and fascinated by the enlightening

information about materials provided by Senior Scientist Frank
Preusser, Mellon Post Doctoral Fellow, Conservation Research,
Rebecca Broyer, and Associate Scientist Charlotte Eng. Fans and
fashion plates were expertly prepared by Senior Conservator and
Head of Paper Conservation Janice Mae Schopfer and her staff,
and Mellon Fellow Erin Jue. Our thanks go also to Leslie Jones,
Associate Curator, and Taras W. Matla, Curatorial Administrator of
the Prints and Drawings Department, for assistance in indentifying
media of works on paper.

The staff of Gallery Services, under the direction of Manager
of Construction William Stahl, rallied with their traditional
dedication and efficiency to the rigorous challenges of the large
and multifaceted exhibition plan. For the labor-intensive and
complicated installation of historic costume and accessories for
Fashioning Fashion: European Dress in Detail, 1700–1915, we extend
heartfelt thanks to Art Preparation and Installation Manager Jeffrey
Haskin and the department's skilled, seasoned, and inventive staff.
Special thanks go to Art Preparator Jeffrey Ono for his ingenious
solutions for custom display mounts.

A significant aspect of LACMA's educational mission is to
engage and inform school-age members of the museum's audience;
to that end, a generous grant to the department from the John B.
and Nelly Llanos Kilroy Foundation was instrumental in the
development of a children's interactive online game that explores
the social and historical context of selected objects in the exhibition.
This intriguing project was realized by Amy Heibel, Manager of
Contemporary Public Programs and New Media, with the help
of freelance writer Susan Hoffman. Our thanks extend to Jane
Burrell, Vice President of Education and Public Programs, and to
Mary Lenihan, Manager of Adult Programs, for the daunting task
of coordinating the R. L. Shep Triennial Symposium for Textiles
and Dress, which focused on European dress of the eighteenth
and nineteenth centuries, and for developing education programs
related to the exhibition *Fashioning Fashion*. For his dedication to
the R. L. Shep Symposium Endowment for Costume and Textiles,
the museum is most grateful to Robb Shep.

As admirers of costume and textiles, we cherish our position as
custodians of the history and heritage of dress. We are honored to
be able to share the museum's opulent collection and are grateful to
donors, colleagues, and friends for their magnanimous support.

Illustration Credits

Most photographs are reproduced courtesy of the creators or lenders of the material depicted. For certain artwork and documentary photographs, we have been unable to locate copyright holders. We would appreciate notification of additional credits for acknowledgment in future editions. Unless otherwise noted, all photographs © 2010 Museum Associates/LACMA.

p. 16: photo © Réunion des Musées Nationaux (MV7850; 93-000747-02) by Gérard Blot/Art Resource, NY (ART392414)

p. 18 (bottom): photo © The Wallace Collection (P418)

p. 19: photo © B.D.V. by Laszlo Veres/Corbis (VE002444)

p. 20 (bottom): photo © Erich Lessing/Art Resource, NY (ART93157)

p. 22 (left): photo by London Stereoscopic Company Comic Series—504/Stringer/Getty Images (2638247)

p. 22 (right): photo © Will Conran/Stringer/Getty Images (2987742)

p. 25 (left): photo © Victoria and Albert Museum, London (Inv.: CAI 3), by Ronald Stoops/Art Resource, NY (ART100268)

p. 25 (right): photo © Library of Congress Online Catalog (LC-USZC2-1978)

p. 27: photo courtesy Museum Associates/LACMA (TT505.P6 I74 1908 [Oversize])

p. 29 (left): photo © Niall McInerney

p. 29 (right): photo © Karl Prouse/Catwalking/Getty Images (84356670)

p. 32 (left): photo © 2010 Freer Gallery of Art and the Arthur M. Sackler Gallery, Smithsonian Institution (F1903.91)

p. 32 (right): photo © Marcio Madeira, courtesy Christian Dior Couture, New York (5565052)

p. 86 (right): published in Dr. Ludovic O'Followell's *Le Corset: histoire, médecine, hygiène: étude historique*, with preface by Paul Ginisty. Published by Maloine (1905), 220. Photo courtesy Wikimedia Commons under Creative Commons Attribution-Share Alike 3.0

p. 94: photo © 2010 The Art Institute of Chicago (1938.1276)

p. 106: © By courtesy of Felix Rosenstiel's Widow & Son Ltd., London, on behalf of the Estate of Sir John Lavery (2002). Photo © Aberdeen Art Gallery & Museums (ABDAG002350)

p. 110: photo © The FORBES Magazine Collection, New York/ The Bridgeman Art Library International (FC 28007)

p. 118 (left): photo © Toulouse, Musée des Augustins, by Daniel Martin (28 01 2005 Ro 618)

p. 156 (bottom): photo © Réunion des Musées Nationaux, Erich Lessing (MV8497)/Art Resource, NY (ART93157)

p. 186 (bottom left): photo © Réunion des Musées Nationaux (MV4390) by Gérard Blot/Art Resource, NY (ART180495)

Index

ALL ILLUSTRATED DRESS AND ACCESSORIES, EXCEPT WHERE OTHERWISE
NOTED, WERE GENEROUSLY PURCHASED WITH FUNDS PROVIDED BY
SUZANNE A. SAPERSTEIN AND MICHAEL AND ELLEN MICHELSON, WITH
ADDITIONAL FUNDING FROM THE COSTUME COUNCIL, THE EDGERTON
FOUNDATION, GAIL AND GERALD OPPENHEIMER, MAUREEN H. SHAPIRO,
GRACE TSAO, AND LENORE AND RICHARD WAYNE

This catalogue was published in conjunction with the exhibition
Fashioning Fashion: European Dress in Detail, 1700–1915, which was
organized by the Los Angeles County Museum of Art

Exhibition Itinerary
Los Angeles County Museum of Art: October 2, 2010–March 6, 2011

Copublished by the
Los Angeles County Museum of Art
5905 Wilshire Boulevard
Los Angeles, CA 90036
lacma.org

and

DelMonico Books, an imprint of Prestel
Prestel, a member of Verlagsgruppe Random House GmbH

Prestel Verlag	Prestel Publishing Ltd.	Prestel Publishing
Königinstrasse 9	4 Bloomsbury Place	900 Broadway, Suite 603
80539 Munich	London WC1A 2QA	New York, NY 10003
Germany	United Kingdom	TEL 212 995 2720
TEL 49 89 242908 300	TEL 44 20 7323 5004	FAX 212 995 2733
FAX 49 89 242908 335	FAX 44 20 7636 8004	sales@prestel-usa.com
prestel.de		prestel.com

© 2010 Museum Associates, Los Angeles County Museum of Art
© 2010 Prestel Verlag, Munich • Berlin • London • New York

Library of Congress Cataloging-in-Publication Data

Takeda, Sharon Sadako.
  Fashioning fashion : European dress in detail, 1700–1915 / Sharon Sadako Takeda
and Kaye Durland Spilker ; with essay by Kimberly Chrisman-Campbell; and
contributions by Kimberly Chrisman-Campbell, Clarissa M. Esguerra, Nicole
LaBouff.
     p. cm.
  Published in conjunction with an exhibition held at the Los Angeles County
Museum of Art. October 2, 2010–March 6, 2011.
  Includes bibliographical references and index.
ISBN: 978-3-7913-5062-2
1. Clothing and dress--Europe--Exhibitions.
2. Costume--Europe--Exhibitions. I. Spilker, Kaye Durland.
II. Chrisman-Campbell, Kimberly. III. Esguerra, Clarissa M. IV. LaBouff, Nicole.
V. Los Angeles County Museum of Art. VI. Title. VII. Title: European dress in
detail, 1700–1915.
  GT720.T35 2010
  391.0074'4--dc22

                                   2010018156

For the Los Angeles County Museum of Art
Head of Publications: Nola Butler
Editor in Chief: Thomas Frick
Editor: Margery L. Schwartz
Editorial Assistant: Monica Paniry
Proofreader: Dianne Woo
Indexer: Kathleen Preciado
Supervising Photographers: Peter Brenner and Steven Oliver
Rights and Reproductions: Cheryle T. Robertson

For DelMonico Books • Prestel
Design: Abbott Miller and Kristen Spilman, Pentagram
Printing and binding: CS Graphics, Singapore

Front cover: Émile Pingat, France, active 1860–1896, *Mantle* (detail), c. 1891
Back cover: *Hunting Jacket* (detail), Scotland, 1825–30